The Cause And Effect Survival Guide

Kelly Logan

Published by Better By Intent Publishing, 2025.

While every precaution has been taken in the preparation of this book, the publisher assumes no responsibility for errors or omissions, or for damages resulting from the use of the information contained herein.

THE CAUSE AND EFFECT SURVIVAL GUIDE

First edition. December 6, 2025.

Copyright © 2025 Kelly Logan.

ISBN: 978-1971255101

Written by Kelly Logan.

Table of Contents

The Cause And Effect Survival Guide 1
CHAPTER 1—The Life You're Living Is the Life You Chose 5
CHAPTER 2—The World Isn't Your Friend (And That's Not Paranoia, It's Math) 9
CHAPTER 3—Pain Doesn't Come From Things—It Comes From You 11
CHAPTER 4—Consequences Are Not Punishments. They're Math. 18
CHAPTER 5—Regret: The Weight You Didn't See Coming 22
CHAPTER 6—Want vs. Worth It: The Choice That Builds Your Future 28
CHAPTER 7—The Power of Pausing: How One Moment Saves You From a Hundred Mistakes 33
CHAPTER 8—Red Flags: Warnings, Not Suggestions 40
CHAPTER 9—The Power of Silence: Your Mouth Doesn't Have to Be an Open Faucet 46
CHAPTER 10—Build Yourself: Skills, Habits, and the Power of Taking Care of Your Own Life 52
CHAPTER 11—Boundaries: Protecting Your Time, Energy, and Sanity 60
CHAPTER 12—Relationships: Choosing People Who Add to Your Life, Not Drain It 67
CHAPTER 13—The Long Game: Building a Future You Can Actually Look Forward To 76
CHAPTER 14—Self-Respect: The Compass That Makes Every Choice Easier 83
CHAPTER 15—Your Environment: The Hidden Force Shaping You Every Day 89
CHAPTER 16—Goals & Direction: How to Move Forward Without Overwhelm 96

CHAPTER 17—Consequences: The Honest Math of Cause and Effect (Where Most People Go Wrong) 103

CHAPTER 18—Temptation & Shiny Objects: How the World Tricks You Into Choosing Regret 110

CHAPTER 19—Emotional Traps: How Your Feelings Trick You Into Bad Decisions 117

CHAPTER 20—The Identity Shift: Becoming Someone Who Chooses Well 125

CHAPTER 21—Personal Responsibility: The Power to Change Your Life Is In Your Hands 132

CHAPTER 22—Stability: Building a Life That Doesn't Fall Apart When Things Get Hard 139

CHAPTER 23—Consistency: The Habit That Changes Everything (Even When You Don't Want To) 146

CHAPTER 24—Self-Control: Pausing, Choosing, and Protecting Your Future 153

CHAPTER 25—Maturity: Growing Into the Version of Yourself You're Meant to Be 160

CHAPTER 26—Healing: Rewriting the Effects of Your Old Choices and Building a Clean Slate 167

CHAPTER 27—Emotional Independence: How to Stop Giving Other People Control Over Your Life 174

CHAPTER 28—Wisdom: Seeing the Long-Term Effects Before You Choose 182

CHAPTER 29—Peace: Designing a Life With Minimal Chaos and Maximum Clarity 189

CHAPTER 30—Your New Life: Living Intentionally by Choosing The Life You Want and Walking Forward Without Fear 196

INTRODUCTION — Before You Make Another Choice

THERE COMES A POINT in life—maybe at 14, maybe at 22, maybe at 47—where you realize something uncomfortable but undeniably true: most of your pain didn't come from fate, or luck, or the universe being dramatic. It came from your choices.

Not because you're dumb or reckless or cursed... but because no one ever taught you how choices actually work.

You grew up in a world full of noise, pressure, shiny distractions, temptations disguised as opportunities, friends who wouldn't know wisdom if it danced naked in front of them, and people who told you what to do without ever telling you what would happen after you did it.

You weren't handed a guidebook.

You were handed chaos.

And then you were expected to "figure it out."

So you did what everyone does:

You guessed.

You reacted.

You followed the crowd.

You went with whatever felt good in the moment.

You listened to whoever spoke the loudest.

You took advice from people whose own lives were on fire.

And then you wondered why everything kept exploding.

This book exists for one reason: to stop you from ruining your life before it starts—or to help you rebuild it if you already started the demolition.

Because here's the truth no one says out loud:

You don't have to hit rock bottom.

You don't have to learn the hard way.

You don't have to lose everything to finally wake up.

You don't have to drown just to learn how to walk on water.
You can learn the cost of a choice before you pay it.
Most people don't know that.
Most people never learn that.
Most people carve entire decades of regret into their lives simply because they didn't stop to ask one simple question:
"If I do this…what will it return to my life?"
See, life isn't random.
It isn't unfair.
It isn't mysterious.
And it definitely isn't about "manifesting" your way out of the damage you did.
Life is cause and effect.
Action→consequence.
Choice→experience.
Impulse→regret.
Awareness→peace.
The problem isn't that you're making choices. The problem is that you were never taught how to see the consequence hiding behind them.
You weren't trained to pause.
You weren't trained to think.
You weren't trained to evaluate outcomes.
You weren't trained to notice the warning signs.
You weren't trained to say no to shiny garbage dressed as opportunity.
You weren't trained to walk away and feel the victory in your chest—that clean, quiet, "Good job…dodged that bullet" grin that blooms when you save yourself.
Instead, you were trained to chase what sparkles…and pay for it later.
This book is your permission slip to choose differently.
To stop hurting yourself.

To stop creating chaos.
To stop living on accident.
And to start building a life you won't need to recover from.

We're going to talk about the consequences no one warns you about:

the kind that break your self-respect, drain your confidence, haunt your mental health, and leave you wondering, "How did I get here?"

We're also going to talk about the peace no one teaches you to protect:

the kind that keeps you stable, steady, safe, and proud of yourself in a way no object, person, or momentary high ever could.

You're going to learn how to:
See the cost of a choice before it hits you
Walk away from people, temptations, and drama without feeling boring or weak
Feel the immediate relief of doing right by yourself
Avoid the traps that ruin lives daily
Protect your future instead of gambling with it
Stop the spiral before it starts
And become the kind of person who gives themselves a quiet, victorious smile for choosing peace over chaos.

And we're going to do it together—with honesty, humor, clarity, and absolutely zero judgment. Because once you understand how cause and effect really works, you'll never fall for the world's tricks again.

You'll walk lighter.
Straighter.
Cleaner.
Smarter.
And with a dignity that can't be shaken.
So take a breath.
This isn't a lecture.
This is your survival guide.

Let's make sure the next chapter of your life is one you actually want to live.

CHAPTER 1—The Life You're Living Is the Life You Chose

Let's get something straight from the start:
Your life didn't "just happen." You didn't trip and fall into your circumstances like a sitcom character who slips on a banana peel. You didn't wake up one morning and find your peace missing like a stolen car.

Life is not random.

Life is not accidental.

Life is not a series of unrelated events strung together by coincidence and "that's just how it goes."

Life is built. One choice at a time.

Not the big choices—everyone knows those matter.

The small ones.

The impulsive ones.

The ones you didn't think counted.

The ones you brushed off with "It's not that serious."

The ones you made because everyone else was doing it.

The ones you made because you wanted to feel something—anything—other than what you were feeling.

The truth is simple and slightly rude:

You are living the accumulation of your choices.

Not your intentions.

Not your excuses.

Not your fantasies.

Not your potential.

Your choices.

Now, before you start feeling called out, let me be clear: You didn't choose most of this consciously. You didn't sit down with a whiteboard and say, "Alright, how can I make my life unnecessarily complicated this month?"

No one does that.

Most of your choices were made while you were half-distracted, under pressure, in pain, in confusion, trying to impress someone, trying to feel better, or trying not to think too hard about the outcome. And that's the problem.

Because choices don't care how you felt when you made them. They don't care if you were tired, emotional, hormonal, stressed, lonely, or trying to avoid disappointment.

Consequences don't check your emotional temperature before arriving.

A choice is a door. Once you walk through it, you're in whatever room it leads to — whether you like the décor or not. You hurt right now not because life is unfair, but because choices return consequences, and some of yours have been...let's say...educational.

This is not judgment. This is cause and effect.

You choose→you experience.

You act→you get a return.

You react→you get a consequence.

You avoid→you still get a consequence.

You ignore→consequences don't.

People love to say, "Everything happens for a reason." Sure. The reason is usually a choice. And when you don't understand how choices work, you end up living in a life you didn't mean to build—with consequences you never wanted, pain you didn't see coming, and regret that sticks to your ribs like wet cement.

That pain you feel?

It's not punishment.

It's not karma targeting you personally.

It's simply the natural outcome of decisions that weren't made with clarity, intention, or awareness.

You weren't taught to pause.
You were taught to react.
You weren't taught to evaluate outcomes.
You were taught to go with the flow.
You weren't taught to say no.
You were taught not to disappoint anyone.
You weren't taught to think ahead.
You were taught to stay in the moment—which is great for breathing exercises but terrible for life choices.

Here's the part most people never realize:

Bad choices don't just create bad moments—they create bad versions of you.

One bad choice makes you feel guilty.
Two bad choices make you feel ashamed.
Three bad choices make you feel hopeless.
Ten bad choices make you believe you are the problem.
Twenty bad choices make you wonder if life even has a future for you.

And in that downward slide, something terrifying happens: You stop trusting yourself. And when you stop trusting yourself, you stop choosing intentionally.

You go numb.
You let life happen to you.
You follow whoever is closest.
You grab at anything that distracts you.
You stop imagining a future.
You think, "What's the point?"
And eventually...you forget you ever had power at all.

But here's the twist—the most important truth in the entire chapter:

If your life is built on choices...then it can be rebuilt with choices.

If choices created the mess, choices can clean it up.
If choices created the regret, choices can create the relief.
If choices built the chaos, choices can build the peace.

And you don't have to wait for a crisis, a rock bottom, or a near-death wakeup call. You can start right now—simply by understanding that every choice is a direction, and every direction leads somewhere. Once you internalize that, everything changes.

You start paying attention.

You start pausing.

You start thinking.

You start considering your future self—the one who has to live with whatever you're about to do. You start learning the pleasure of walking away clean, whispering, "Good job... dodged that bullet." You begin walking through your life instead of stumbling through it.

This chapter isn't here to shame you. It's here to give you your power back—by making you aware of something you've never been taught:

Your life isn't happening to you. It's happening because of you.

And that means you can change it. One intentional choice at a time.

CHAPTER 2—The World Isn't Your Friend (And That's Not Paranoia, It's Math)

Before we go any further, let's clear up one of the biggest misunderstandings you were raised with:
the world is not here to help you.
Not because it hates you.
Not because you're unlucky.
Not because there's some cosmic vendetta with your name on it.

But because the world has one job—to keep you distracted, impulsive, overwhelmed, emotional, and chasing things that feel good for five minutes and ruin your life for five years.

And it's very, very good at its job. The world hands you shiny objects like candy at a parade:
"Look! Fun! Exciting! Everyone else is doing it! You deserve this! Don't think—just take it!"

And because you're human—because you want connection, excitement, validation, pleasure, relief, belonging—you reach for it.

You don't see the trap until you're already in it.

This isn't about being paranoid.

This is about recognizing patterns so obvious you'll wonder why no one told you sooner.

The world does not run on wisdom.

It runs on **impulse**. And impulse is the exact opposite of peace.

Let's look at how this works:

The Shiny Object→Regret Pipeline

Every mistake in your life started the same way:
something looked good.
Not "was good."
Not "aligned with who you want to become."
Not "beneficial."

Just...shiny.

The world is FULL of shiny things:
-people who look exciting but are walking disasters
-opportunities that are really traps
-trends that drain your dignity
-temptations that feel like a secret doorway to fun
-relationships that flatter your loneliness
-decisions that promise pleasure now and deliver pain later

And the world counts on you being too distracted, too emotional, or too curious to stop and ask:

"What happens after this?" Because the world is built on bait-and-switch.

The bait: pleasure.

The switch: consequences.

The problem isn't that temptation exists—temptation is unavoidable.

The problem is you **weren't taught how to see the cost behind the sparkle.**

So you go for the gold...and end up with glitter glued to a turd.

CHAPTER 3—Pain Doesn't Come From Things—It Comes From You

People spend an incredible amount of time blaming the wrong things for their misery.

They blame their job, their parents, their partner, their lack of sleep, their bank account, their childhood, their boss, their schedule, their zodiac sign... anything within arm's reach.

But here's the unglamorous truth nobody advertises:

Pain doesn't come from things—it comes from the choices you make around those things.

Not because everything is your fault, but because your wellbeing depends on how you respond, not what shows up. This isn't about blame. This is about understanding the mechanics.

Most people live in reaction mode.

Something happens→they react.

Someone says something→they react.

A feeling hits→they react.

A temptation appears→they react.

And reactions, especially fast ones, rarely lead to peace. Let's break it into simple cause-and-effect.

• • • •

You Can't Fix Internal Problems With External Solutions

WHENEVER YOU FEEL UNHAPPY or uncomfortable, the world offers you quick fixes:
- -buy something
- -eat something
- -post something
- -date someone

-escape into entertainment
-stay busy
-numb out

Those things can distract you, but they cannot fix you because the discomfort you're trying to escape usually came from choices—not circumstances.

If you keep choosing:
-people who drain you
-habits that stress you
-situations that don't support you
-impulses that backfire
-distractions that postpone problems

...you're going to feel the consequences no matter how many treats, gadgets, nights out, or "new beginnings" you throw at it. **Pain isn't random. It's feedback.** You're not being punished—you're being informed.

• • • •

Why the Emptiness Keeps Returning

HERE'S THE SIMPLEST pattern most people never notice: Bad choices don't instantly ruin your life—they slowly chip away at how you feel about yourself.

One small chip doesn't do much. But dozens? Now you feel off-center and can't figure out why.

Examples:
You say yes when you want to say no→resentment
You ignore red flags→stress
You procrastinate→anxiety
You gossip→embarrassment
You keep secrets→tension
You stay somewhere you've outgrown→exhaustion

Each one seems minor... until they pile up. This is why people wake up one day and feel "off," "numb," "lost," or "unmotivated." Not because something huge happened—but because little consequences added up. It's not dramatic. It's math.

• • • •

One Choice Doesn't Break You—But Repetition Will

ANYONE CAN MAKE ONE bad call. That's human. The problem is what happens after. Most people go:

"Well, I already messed up...might as well keep going." That's how one bad decision becomes a streak.

And streaks become patterns.

Patterns create outcomes.

And outcomes create how you feel about yourself.

This is the real reason people slide into low motivation, low mood, low confidence—not because life attacked them, but because quiet choices added up quietly. You don't need a deep psychological dive to understand it. You just need to notice the sequence.

• • • •

The Most Common Cause of Self-Inflicted Pain

IGNORING SIGNALS.

Ignoring the feeling in your chest.

Ignoring the tension.

Ignoring the dread.

Ignoring your own limits.

Ignoring the obvious outcome.

Ignoring what you already know you should do

Ignore enough of these, and life gets heavy.

Not because you're broken—because you're bypassing your own common sense.

Ignoring yourself is the easiest way to end up in situations you never needed to experience.

• • • •

The Exit Isn't Complicated

IF THE PAIN CAME FROM choices, then peace comes from choices. Not dramatic choices. Not life-changing declarations. Not a whole new personality.

Just steady, simple decisions like:
-pausing before reacting
-walking away sooner
-choosing people who treat you well
-doing what you said you'd do
-passing on the shiny things that cost too much later
-being honest
-keeping your space clean
-saying no when something feels wrong

Every one of those returns something positive back to you. The moment you start choosing better—even a little—you feel better. And yes, sometimes you'll walk away from something and feel that little spark of pride rise in your chest. That quiet, victorious **"You did good!"**

That feeling?

That's the return on a good decision.

Pain isn't destiny. It's just the outcome of choices that weren't working for you. And peace works the same way—it's built. Choice by choice.

"Try it, it's not a big deal"
"Post it—it'll get likes"

"They won't find out"
"We're all doing it"
"Come on, don't be that person"
Translation: **"Don't think. Don't pause. Don't weigh the future. Just react."** And that, right there, is how most people ruin their lives.
Not by being evil.
Not by being stupid.
Not by being doomed.
Just by being too afraid to stand alone and think.

Here's a secret only wise people know: **Anyone who pressures you to be reckless isn't your friend—they're your liability.** And the world is full of liabilities.

• • • •

Marketing: The World's Legalized Manipulation Industry

NOT EVERYTHING THAT manipulates you is human. Most of it is digital. Entire corporations exist for one reason: to make you want things you didn't want, need things you don't need, buy things you can't afford, and feel inferior so they can sell you the "fix."

Social media? Engineered to keep you addicted. Every scroll is psychological bait.

Advertisements? Crafted to make your brain feel like you're missing out. They want your attention, your insecurity, your impulse purchases—not your wellbeing.

Trends? Created to make you feel outdated if you don't participate. You get sucked into spending to avoid feeling "less."

None of this has anything to do with your future peace, your mental health, or your long-term happiness. The world doesn't think ahead for you. That's your job.

• • • •

The Illusion of "Everyone Else Is Doing It"

HERE'S A TRUTH BOMB the world hides under a rug: **Most people are not doing well.**
    They're not happy.
    They're not stable.
    They're not peaceful.
    They're not making good choices.
    They're not thriving.
    They're not building a future.
    They're just loud.
    And because humans imitate what's around them, you mistakenly assume the crowd knows where it's going. **The crowd has no idea where it's going,** it just hates feeling lonely, so it moves together. If you follow the crowd, you get the crowd's life—which is usually a mess held together by denial and duct tape.

• • • •

You Don't Have to Play This Game

THIS CHAPTER IS MEANT to help you see the game for what it is:
    The world benefits when you don't think, don't pause, don't choose—you just react.
    But you are not a puppet.
    You are not a follower.
    And you are not obligated to participate in your own destruction just because everyone else is.
    The moment you learn to stop, to pause, to see beyond the shiny surface, you become immune to 90% of the world's nonsense. You start walking around with a kind of calm, grounded confidence that makes you untouchable. People can tempt you, pressure you, provoke you, distract you—and you just... don't bite.

Because you're thinking long-term.
You're protecting your peace.
You're building a life, not chasing a moment.

And you're starting to understand the most important truth in this entire chapter:

The world can only control you when you don't control yourself. And that ends now.

CHAPTER 4—Consequences Are Not Punishments. They're Math.

Most people talk about consequences like they're some cosmic slap on the wrist. They'll say things like "It's karma," "It's fate," "The universe is testing me," or "I just can't catch a break."

No. Stop right there.

Consequences are not personal. They're not emotional. They're not spiritual revenge.

Consequences are math.

Do X→get Y.

Make a choice→get a return.

Not punishment. Not payback. Just results. Let's look at how this works.

• • • •

Most people see the action and forget the return.

ACTION: You lie to avoid conflict.
Return: You feel guilty and now you have to maintain the lie.
Action: You skip an assignment because you're tired.
Return: Stress and a bigger problem tomorrow.
Action: You date someone who's "fine, I guess."
Return: Emotional confusion and second-guessing.
Action: You post something impulsive.
Return: Permanent digital awkwardness.
Predictable. Not personal.

• • • •

THE CAUSE AND EFFECT SURVIVAL GUIDE 19

The Return Usually Arrives Quietly

CONSEQUENCES DON'T always show up as disasters. They show up as:
- A tightening in your chest
- A little dread
- Guilt or tension
- A messy feeling you can't shake
- That "ugh, I didn't need to do that" moment.
- Quiet consequences ignored eventually become loud ones.

• • • •

Intent Matters—But Results Matter More

YOU MAY NOT *mean* to cause problems, but consequences respond to the action, not the intention.
  Action: You accidentally overshare.
  Return: Now your privacy is compromised.
  Action: You accidentally take on too much.
  Return: You burn out.
  Action: You trust another more than yourself
  Return: You suffer the consequences
  It's not punishment. It's just what happens.
  Predictability=control.
  Control=peace.

• • • •

Short-Term Relief vs Long-Term Reality

SHORT-TERM COMFORT almost always costs long-term peace.
  Short-term: Avoid the hard talk.

Return: Long-term tension.
Short-term: Say yes when you want to say no.
Return: Long-term resentment.
Short-term: Stay in the familiar relationship.
Return: Long-term emotional drain.
Short-term: Take the temptation.
Return: Long-term regret.
It's basic math.

• • • •

The Chain Reaction Effect

ONE CHOICE CAN START a domino line.

Action: You avoid a task→**Return**: stress→**Action:** stress makes you avoid more→**Return**: bigger mess.

Action: You lie→**Return**: guilt→**Action:** guilt creates avoidance→**Return**: damaged trust.

It's not "your life falling apart." **It's patterns stacking.**

• • • •

Understanding the Math Brings Calm

ONCE YOU SEE THE PATTERN, life stops feeling chaotic or unfair and starts feeling:
Logical
Manageable
Predictable
Steady

Your choices shape outcomes—not your worth, your intentions, or your luck. And outcomes can change anytime you change the choices.

• • • •

The Best Part? You Control the Equation

WHEN YOU UNDERSTAND cause and effect, you can use it. You can:
    Pause before reacting
    See the return before you choose
    Avoid obvious traps
    Pick people who support your peace
    Solve small problems before they grow
    Walk away early
    Make choices with long-term payoff
    Consequences stop being surprises and start being information. Signals. Data. Your life becomes something you direct—not something you survive.
    One choice.
    One equation.
    One return at a time.

CHAPTER 5—Regret: The Weight You Didn't See Coming

Most people think regret comes from one big, dramatic mistake—the kind you see in movies.
In real life? Regret usually comes from something much smaller:
One moment of impulse
One decision made under pressure
One "I'll deal with this later"
One shiny temptation that looked harmless
One choice you didn't pause to think through
Regret doesn't feel like a slap.
It feels like a slow leak.
A little loss of confidence here.
A little self-disappointment there.
A quiet "I knew better" in the background of your mind.
It builds quietly, quietly, quietly...until one day it's heavy enough that you finally feel it. This chapter will show you what regret really is—so you can avoid it before it ever forms.

• • • •

Regret Usually Starts Small

MOST REGRET DOESN'T begin with a dramatic explosion. It begins with a tiny moment you brushed off:
Action: You ignore a red flag.
Return: Now you're emotionally tangled.
Action: You follow the crowd.
Return: You end up with a consequence the group won't help you fix.
Action: You take the temptation because it feels fun.

Return: You deal with the fallout alone.
Action: You avoid the thing you know you should do.
Return: You create bigger problems for your future self.
Regret is not a single moment.
It's a collection of "I wish I hadn't" woven together over time.

• • • •

Regret Hits Hard Because It's Doesn't Play Games

YOU CAN ARGUE WITH guilt.
    You can justify bad choices.
    You can distract yourself from discomfort.
    But regret? Regret doesn't negotiate.
    Regret shows up with:
    Clarity
    Honesty
    No sugarcoating
    No excuses
    No confusion
    It's the moment you recognize your own role in your own pain. That sounds heavy, but it's actually empowering—because it means regret is preventable.

• • • •

The Mental Weight of Regret

REGRET IS HEAVY BECAUSE it affects how you see yourself. It creates:
    Self-doubt
    Hesitation
    Overthinking

Second-guessing
Loss of confidence
Emotional fog
The feeling that you "can't trust yourself"

This is the real damage—not the situation itself, but what it does to your identity. When you accumulate regret, you start living smaller.

More cautiously.
More anxiously.

Not because life is dangerous...but because you're scared of your own decision-making. That's the part people never talk about.

• • • •

Why Regret Will Spiral if You Ignore It

REGRET CREATES DISCOMFORT.
Discomfort looks for an escape.
The escape is usually another bad choice.
And now you're in the same spiral we talked about earlier, just from a different angle:

Regret→avoidance→distraction→impulse→new regret.

This is how people end up in cycles that get heavier over time.
Not because they're doomed.
Not because they're broken.
But because no one taught them how to break the pattern.
You're learning that now.

• • • •

The Overlooked Cost of Regret: Energy

REGRET DRAINS YOUR focus.
It drains your motivation.

It drains your ability to look forward.
It drains your excitement about the future.
Regret **affects** you mentally and physically. It becomes:
The pain in your body
Depression/Low self esteem
Substance abuse/inability to control emotions
The voices inside your head that beats you daily

Most people don't realize regret is what's draining life right out of them. This is why you hear people say they feel "tired as a person."

It's not age. It's accumulated regret like a mountain suffocating them slowly.

• • • •

Regret Isn't your punishment—It's the lesson you are supposed to learn from

HERE'S THE IMPORTANT thing:

Regret isn't some moral punishment. It's just the natural result of choices you didn't think through.

You weren't bad. You were unprepared.

Regret teaches you what you need to know **before** you do the thing the next time. Once you understand this, regret becomes a teacher—not an enemy.

Regret is a hot stove...and you now know how not to get burned.

• • • •

You Don't Need to Hit Rock Bottom to Learn

THE WORLD LOVES SELLING the "rise from the ashes" story.
Rock bottom.
Turning point.

Phoenix moment.
You don't need any of that.
You don't need to crash your life to understand it.
You don't need to drown to learn to swim.
You don't have to get hurt to grow.
You can learn in advance.
You can think ahead.
You can pause.
You can see the return before the action.
You can walk away clean.
That's the whole point of this book. Regret is optional. Not because you'll be perfect—but because you'll be aware.

• • • •

How Regret Can Protect You (If You Let It)

REGRET BECOMES USEFUL once you understand what it's saying.
It's not "You're terrible."
It's "You didn't choose what was good for you."
It's not "You're broken."
It's "You didn't think far enough ahead."
It's not "Your life is doomed."
It's "You can do better next time."
And when you do better next time, something incredible happens: You get that clean, proud, private feeling. That internal nod.
That "good job buddy! Another one in the win column!" warmth in your chest.
That feeling is the opposite of regret. It's self-respect.
And once you taste that just a few times...you'll do anything to feel it again.

• • • •

Regret Is Not a Life Sentence—It's a Signal

REGRET IS JUST INFORMATION: "This wasn't worth the cost."

Once you understand the cost before you act, you stop choosing things you'll regret later. The whole goal of this chapter is simple:

Learn the cost in advance.
Learn the consequences in advance.
Learn the return in advance.

You control regret by controlling the cause—not by beating yourself up after. And now you know how.

CHAPTER 6—Want vs. Worth It: The Choice That Builds Your Future

If you can master this chapter, you can navigate almost anything life throws at you. Because every choice you make sits at the crossroads of two simple questions:

Do I want this? And **Is it worth it?**

Most people only answer the first one. They see something they want—attention, fun, temptation, validation, escape, approval, comfort—and they act on it without asking the second question. That's where the trouble begins.

You can want something with your whole heart, but that doesn't make it worth the consequences that come attached. Let's make this simple and practical.

• • • •

WANT=THE FEELING YOU have right now.
Worth it=the reality you'll live with later.
Those two are rarely the same. Examples:
Want: To clap back in a heated moment.
Worth it: Not really—now you've created drama you didn't need.
Want: To skip something important because you're tired.
Worth it: No—tomorrow will hit twice as hard.
Want: To say yes so no one is disappointed.
Worth it: Not when it drains you and builds resentment.
Want: To go out with someone who excites you.
Worth it: If all they bring is chaos, excitement is not enough.

This is the cleanest, simplest way to protect your future: **Ask "Is it worth it?" before you say yes to what you want.**

• • • •

The Trick the World Plays on You

THE WORLD TRAINS YOU to chase what you want, not what's worth it. Everything from ads to social pressure to entertainment is built around feeding desire:

Want fun?
Want attention?
Want love?
Want a break?
Want to feel good for five minutes?
Want to forget your problems?

The world hands you shiny objects on a conveyor belt. But none of these systems care what happens after. Want is easy. Worth it takes thinking. The world counts on you **not** thinking.

• • • •

Wants Feel Big. Consequences Hit Harder.

WHEN YOU WANT SOMETHING, your brain begins to **rationalize**:

"This will feel good."
"This will be fun."
"I deserve this."
"Whatever, it's fine."
"Other people do it."
"It's not that serious."

But consequences aren't fantasy, **they are reality and affect:**
Your time
Your energy
Your future
Your pride
Your mental health

Your peace
Your goals
Your self-respect
That's why people get blindsided.

Want is short-term in the moment, temporary enjoyment.

Worth it is long-term permanent peace because you didn't add consequences.

Short-term wins usually have long-term consequences.

• • • •

If You Can Pause, You Win

YOU DON'T NEED SPECIAL skills.

You don't need perfect discipline.

You don't need to become a monk.

You only need **a pause.** A three to five-second pause is enough to switch from emotion to logic:

"Do I want this because it helps me...or because it helps me escape something?"

"Is the return on this action worth living with?"

"Will I be proud of this later?"

"Will this create regret...or relief?"

That tiny moment is where your power lives.

• • • •

The Most Common Wants That Aren't Worth It

WANT: To impress someone.
  Worth it: Usually not. People forget quickly; consequences don't.
  Want: Attention from the wrong person.
  Worth it: Never. The cost is always higher than the thrill.

Want: To respond emotionally.
Worth it: Almost never—you can't take words back.
Want: To fit in.
Worth it: Not when it requires shrinking yourself.
Want: To avoid discomfort.
Worth it: Discomfort avoided becomes chaos multiplied.
Want: To chase fun without thinking.
Worth it: Only when fun doesn't wreck your peace.
Again, not moral judgments—just simple cause and effect.

• • • •

Worth It Choices Build Self-Respect

EVERY TIME YOU CHOOSE what's worth it instead of what you want in the moment, something important happens: You trust yourself a little more.

You feel steadier.

You feel clearer.

You feel proud of yourself in that quiet, warm way—the one that feels like your chest lights up from the inside.

It's that internal pat on the back.

That grin and the whisper of "Good job" within.

That feeling is worth more than anything you could get from chasing a want because wants disappear but **self-respect is of you.** It is the only thing in this life that means anything to your happiness and is the only thing that cannot be taken from you by the world.

• • • •

What You Want Will Change. What's Worth It Rarely Does.

YOUR WANTS WILL SHIFT daily:

Stress wants escape
Loneliness wants attention
Boredom wants chaos
Insecurity wants validation
Hurt wants retaliation
Excitement wants risk
But things that are worth it? They're consistent.
Peace is worth it.
Safety is worth it.
Health is worth it.
Dignity is worth it.
Time is worth it.
Mental clarity is worth it.
Avoiding regret is worth it.
A future that feels stable is worth it.
Your self-respect is worth it every single time.
That's the equation: Wants change fast.
What is worth it doesn't.

• • • •

The Goal Isn't to Stop Wanting—It's to Stop Paying Too Much

YOU'RE NEVER GOING to stop wanting things. Want is human. But awareness makes the difference:

"I can want this...**without** choosing it."

That's maturity. That's power. That's emotional independence. And it's how you build a life that doesn't fall apart every time a shiny object walks by.

Wants pull you.
Worth-it choices **build** you.
And you're learning to choose the second one.

CHAPTER 7—The Power of Pausing: How One Moment Saves You From a Hundred Mistakes

If you learn nothing else from this book—nothing, not one single concept—learn **this**:
A pause is the difference between a peaceful life and a chaotic one.
Not a meditation retreat.
Not deep therapy work.
Not a personality overhaul.
Just…a pause.
One beat.
One breath.
One moment where you don't react automatically.
This is the smallest skill with the biggest return. Let's break it down.

• • • •

Most Mistakes Come From Speed, Not Stupidity

PEOPLE DON'T USUALLY ruin their lives because they're careless or reckless. They ruin their lives because they act **too fast**.
Fast reactions lead to:
Emotional texts
Impulsive choices
Agreeing when you don't want to
Snapping when you're stressed
Grabbing the shiny object
Ignoring red flags
Saying things you can't take back
Acting from pressure instead of intention

Choosing relief over logic
Speed is the enemy of peace. A pause brings the speed down to something human—something deliberate.

• • • •

A Pause Interrupts the Consequence Pipeline

EVERY CHOICE HAS A pattern:
Impulse→Pause→Action→Consequence

If you don't pause, you go straight from impulse→action. That's where chaos lives. But when you pause—even two seconds—something magical happens: You actually see the action before you make it.

You see the return.

You see the consequence.

You see the future version of you dealing with whatever you're about to do.

That two-second window gives you your whole life back.

• • • •

Pausing Lets Your Future Self Into the Conversation

WHEN YOU DON'T PAUSE, your current self is the only one voting.

And current-you is:

Emotional

Tired

Stressed

Bored

Annoyed

Tempted

Under pressure
Wanting something quick
Wanting something easy
Wanting something now
But future-you? Future-you is the one who has to pay the bill. A pause gives future-you a chance to speak up:
"Hey...can we **not** do this? I'm the one who has to deal with it."
Instant wisdom. Hardship avoided all because you took a beat to think.

• • • •

A Pause Is Not "Doing Nothing"—It's Doing the Smartest Possible Thing

PEOPLE THINK PAUSING means you're weak, unsure, or awkward. Not true.
A pause is strategy.
It's control.
It's clarity.
The quietest person in the room—the one who takes a beat before speaking—is almost always perceived as the most intelligent. Why? Because they think before they act.
A pause doesn't make you slow it makes you effective.

• • • •

Pausing Makes You Look Smarter, Kinder, and More Confident

WANT TO INSTANTLY APPEAR more grounded?
More mature?
More self-respecting?
More in control?

Pause.
Before answering a question.
Before reacting to something emotional.
Before saying yes.
Before saying no.
Before hitting send.
Before taking someone home.
Before walking into drama.
Before doing anything you know could cost you later.
People who pause:
Don't overshare
Don't escalate situations
Don't embarrass themselves
Don't reveal their insecurities
Don't let others steer them
Don't get sucked into nonsense
Don't create fires they later have to put out
A pause is power disguised as silence.

• • • •

A Pause Isn't Awkward—It's Strategic

THE WORLD TRAINED YOU to fear silence.
 To fill every quiet moment.
 To respond instantly.
 To keep the conversation going.
But here's the truth:
Silence makes people listen.
Silence makes people reveal themselves.
Silence makes you seem calm and collected.
Silence gives you time to think.
Silence gives you the advantage.

A pause is not dead air—it's breathing room. It's the moment where clarity enters.

• • • •

Pausing Protects You From Yourself

MOST OF THE CONSEQUENCES you've lived through weren't caused by evil plans or massive mistakes — they were caused by reacting too fast.

A pause protects you from:
Your emotions
Your impulses
Your stress
Your defensiveness
Your habits
Your overthinking
Your people-pleasing
Your fear of missing out

Imagine how many situations could have been avoided if you paused:
The fight?
The bad date?
The embarrassing text?
The oversharing?
The regret?
The money spent on impulse?
The drama you walked into?
All preventable.

• • • •

The Easiest Way to Pause (No One Will Know You Are Doing It)

HERE'S A SIMPLE FORMULA you can memorize:
Pause→Breathe→Think→Decide.
That's it.
Pause: Interrupt the speed.
Breathe: Reset your brain.
Think: "What does this bring back into my life?"
Decide: Not react—**decide**.
This takes seconds. Not minutes. Seconds. And it saves you hours, days, even years of consequences.

• • • •

The More You Pause, the Stronger You Feel

THIS IS WHERE IT GETS fun. The more you pause, the more you notice:
"I don't actually want this."
"This isn't worth it."
"This would have caused regret."
"That's not my problem."
"That's not my responsibility."
"That's not my future."
And the more you say no to things that aren't worth it, the more you start feeling:
Clear
Solid
Mature
Confident
Calm
Powerful
Proud of yourself

That feeling never gets old—the internal grin after walking away from something harmful. That's the **reward**.

• • • •

A Pause Makes You the Author, Not the Audience

WHEN YOU REACT INSTANTLY, life writes over you. When you pause, **you write your own script.**

You stop being pulled by emotion.

You stop being dragged by other people's demands.

You stop getting caught in situations you never meant to be in.

You become the one making the choices—not the one cleaning them up.

And that, my friend, is the foundation of a steady, peaceful, intentional life.

CHAPTER 8—Red Flags: Warnings, Not Suggestions

If there's one universal truth about life, it's this:
   Red flags never get smaller.
They don't fade.
They don't fix themselves.
They don't turn green if you squint.
And they definitely don't disappear just because you want them to.
A red flag is not a suggestion.
It's not a maybe.
It's not a "might be nothing."
A red flag is a forecast. And here's the part that saves lives:
Red flags always show up early, long before anything major happens.

But most people ignore them because the beginning feels good, exciting, convenient, or comfortable. This chapter is about learning to see red flags as **information**, not drama—because once you treat red flags the way they're meant to be treated, you avoid 80% of preventable pain.

Let's break it down.

• • • •

A Red Flag Is Not an Accident—It's Data

A RED FLAG IS SIMPLY a piece of early evidence that something won't end well. Predictable problems always make early appearances. Always.

Examples:
Red flag: Someone gets irritated when you set a boundary.
Return: They will not respect your needs.

Red flag: Someone talks badly about everyone in their life.
Return: You'll be next.
Red flag: Someone is great at fun but terrible at responsibility.
Return: You'll end up carrying the weight.
Red flag: Someone makes excuses instead of progress.
Return: You'll be drained waiting for change that isn't coming.
Red flags aren't mysterious. **They're previews.**

• • • •

Why People Ignore Red Flags (The Honest List)

PEOPLE DON'T IGNORE red flags because they're blind. They ignore them because they're hopeful.

Or lonely.
Or insecure.
Or bored.
Or craving excitement.
Or afraid of walking away.
Or tired of starting over.
Or desperate for a connection. Or worried there won't be something better.

Here's the truth: **Ignoring a red flag does not make the problem go away. It makes the consequences come faster.**

Red flags are the universe handing you a memo saying, "Hey...if you continue, here's the price."

• • • •

Red Flags Don't Predict the Moment—They Predict the Pattern

A SINGLE MOMENT IS small. A pattern is everything.
Red flag: Someone's rude to the waiter.

Pattern: They disrespect people with less power.
Red flag: They can't apologize.
Pattern: They cannot take accountability—ever.
Red flag: They flirt with everyone.
Pattern: They need external validation constantly.
Red flag: They talk over you.
Pattern: They don't value you.

The moment is tiny—but the pattern is the structure your future is built on. This is why horizontal thinkers walk away early: They understand the moment is just the sample size.

• • • •

A Red Flag You Ignore Now Becomes the Problem You Live With Later

THIS IS SIMPLE CAUSE and effect.

Ignore the red flag→deal with the fallout→Walk away early→avoid the fallout altogether.

People think walking away is dramatic.

It's **not**.

It's preventative.

Drama isn't caused by walking away. Drama is caused by staying when everything is telling you to go.

• • • •

Red Flags Aren't Just for People—They Apply Everywhere

JOBS.
Friendships.
Choices.
Opportunities.

Habits.
Commitments.
Plans.
Financial decisions.
Even environments.
Examples:
Red flag: Job feels chaotic on day one.
Return: It's not going to magically become organized.
Red flag: A "once in a lifetime" opportunity pressures you to act fast.
Return: If it's real, it won't require panic.
Red flag: A habit steals your time or focus.
Return: It's headed toward addiction territory.
Red flag: A friend disappears when you need them.
Return: They're not dependable.
Same pattern everywhere: Red flag→early warning→final outcome.

• • • •

The Most Revealing Red Flag: Your Own Discomfort

YOU DON'T NEED SOMEONE to behave terribly to feel a red flag. Sometimes the red flag is simply:
  You feel uneasy
  You feel pressured
  You feel off
  You feel rushed
  You feel drained
  You feel unsettled
  You feel small
  You feel obligated
  You feel guilty for wanting space

Your body notices things your mind hasn't named yet. A red flag doesn't need a long explanation. You don't have to justify it. You don't need evidence. **Your discomfort is the evidence.**

• • • •

You Don't Need to Fight Red Flags—You Just Need to Pause

THIS IS WHERE WHAT you have learned so far starts to connect.
A pause gives you the space to ask:
"Is this worth the cost?"
"What is this red flag predicting?"
"What would future-me say about this?"
"Do I feel grounded or off-balance?"
"Does this benefit my life or complicate it?"
You don't need to confront the person.
You don't need to fix them.
You don't need to give a long speech.
You just need to acknowledge the data and adjust accordingly.

• • • •

Red Flags Help You Avoid Regret, Not Connection

PEOPLE THINK WALKING away means you're cold, closed-off, or judgmental. No.
Walking away early is:
Responsible
Wise
Protective
Mature
Mentally healthy
Time-saving

Energy-saving
Self-respecting
You're not rejecting people. You're rejecting predictable pain. That's not rude. That's **intelligent**.

• • • •

Your New Rule: One Red Flag=Awareness. Two=Decision. Three=Done.

ONE RED FLAG? YOU OBSERVE.
Two red flags? You pause and evaluate the return.
Three red flags? You're out.
No drama.
No debate.
No negotiating with potential.
This keeps your life clean.
Light.
Steady.
Peaceful.
Because you're no longer hoping people will be different than they're showing you. You're taking them at face value—and choosing accordingly.

CHAPTER 9—The Power of Silence: Your Mouth Doesn't Have to Be an Open Faucet

Silence is one of the strongest skills you can have—and one of the rarest. Not because people don't like silence, but because people fear it.

They fear being misunderstood.
They fear looking weak.
They fear missing their chance to speak up.
They fear that if they don't explain themselves, they'll lose control of the situation.

But here's the truth: **Silence gives you more control than talking ever will.**

Not the silent treatment.
Not manipulation.
Not passive-aggressive withholding.

We're talking about **intentional silence**—the kind that creates space for clarity, self-respect, and smart decisions.

• • • •

Talking Fast=Acting Fast

MOST PEOPLE TALK THE way they react:
  Too quickly
  Too emotionally
  Too defensively
  Too unfiltered
  Too revealing
  Too much

Almost every regretful comment starts with speed—the urge to fill the air before the other person fills it for you. Silence breaks that pattern.

A pause before speaking is the conversational version of a seatbelt. It keeps you safe.

• • • •

Silence Makes You Look More Confident (Even if You're Not)

THERE'S A REASON THE quietest person in a group often comes across as the most intelligent.

Silence signals:
Composure
Thinking
Awareness
Control
Maturity
Presence

Talking too much—especially too fast—signals the opposite. People who speak slowly, simply, and intentionally give off a calm authority.

They don't overshare.
They don't bury themselves with words.
They don't reveal insecurities.
They don't sound frantic.

And the best part? You don't have to try. **Silence does the work for you.**

• • • •

Silence Keeps You From Making the Situations Worse

A LOT OF DRAMA STARTS with someone saying 10 words more than they needed to. A lot of relationships end because someone talked past the point of clarity. A lot of friendships get strained because someone kept explaining, defending, or elaborating when silence would've landed better.

Silence protects you from:
Overexplaining
Defending yourself unnecessarily
Sharing personal details too soon
Responding emotionally
Escalating tension
Sounding guilty
Sounding insecure
Silence keeps the unnecessary consequences away.

• • • •

Silence Gives You Time to Think

TALKING FILLS SPACE. Silence creates space. And that space is where your best decisions come from.

A quick mental checklist:
Pause→breathe→think→then speak.
Most people speak in the "impulse" phase.
Silence lets you speak in the "decision" phase.
It's not awkward—**it's strategic.**

• • • •

Not Everything Needs a Reaction

HERE'S THE TRUTH THAT frees you: **You are not required to respond to everything.**
    Not every question.
    Not every comment.
    Not every message.
    Not every accusation.
    Not every invitation.
    Not every provocation.
    Not every piece of gossip.
    Not every emotional dump.
    Most people talk because they feel obligated. You don't have to. Silence is a boundary in sound form.

• • • •

Silence Protects Your Privacy

OVERSHARING FEELS GOOD in the moment, but it comes with a cost:
    People form opinions
    People use your words against you
    People spread your business
    People misunderstand you
    People expect more access than you want to give
    Silence—intentional silence—keeps your life clean.
    You decide what people know.
    You decide what people don't know.
    You decide what's sacred.
    You decide what's safe.
    Your privacy is power.

· · · ·

Silence Gives Other People Space to Reveal Themselves

HERE'S ONE OF THE MOST powerful truths: **When you stay quiet, other people talk. And when they talk, they reveal everything.**

Silence pulls information out of people:
their intentions
their honesty
their character
their insecurities
their motives
their plans

People fill silence with who they are. You learn more by listening quietly than by speaking loudly.

· · · ·

Silence Keeps You From Being Reactive

WHEN YOU PAUSE, YOU'RE choosing: "I'm not letting the moment decide for me."

Silence protects you from:
Snapping
Sarcasm
Panic responses
Emotional spills
Saying things you can't take back
Defensive explanations
That awful "Why did I say that?" feeling

It's not that you don't have something to say. It's that you're choosing when, how, and if you say it. That's a whole different kind of strength.

• • • •

Silence Is Not Withdrawal—It's Wisdom

SILENCE DOESN'T MEAN ignoring someone. It doesn't mean shutting down. It doesn't mean bottling things up.

It means you:
Think before you speak
Protect yourself
Choose your moment
Choose your tone
Choose your direction

Silence is an intentional step, not avoidance. It's you choosing clarity over chaos.

• • • •

Your New Rule: Speak with Intention, Not Impulse

A SIMPLE STANDARD TO live by:
If speaking helps, speak.
If speaking complicates things, pause.
If speaking exposes you, stay silent.
If speaking drains you, stay quiet.
If speaking is pressure, delay.
If speaking is impulse, wait.
Your mouth doesn't have to be an open faucet.
Control the flow. Control the outcome.

CHAPTER 10—Build Yourself: Skills, Habits, and the Power of Taking Care of Your Own Life

If you want independence—real independence—you need more than confidence, awareness, and good decision-making. You need **skills**.

Not fancy skills.
Not resume skills.
Not "impress other people" skills.
Life skills. The kind that make your daily existence easier, cleaner, healthier, calmer, and more self-respecting. People underestimate how much their basic habits impact their mental health.

But here's the truth: **You feel better about your life when you can take care of yourself.**

And you feel terrible when you can't.

This chapter is about building the foundation—the boring, unglamorous skills that secretly determine whether your life feels smooth or chaotic.

• • • •

Taking Care of Yourself Is Not a Chore—It's Identity Formation

WHEN YOU CONSISTENTLY handle your own responsibilities, something subtle happens:

You start to trust yourself.
You start to feel capable.
You start to recognize your own competence.
You start to feel stable.

That stability is emotional gold. It carries into every area of life. And when you don't handle your responsibilities? Your identity wobbles.

You feel embarrassed.
You feel behind.
You feel unprepared.
You feel dependent.
You feel overwhelmed.
You feel like you're always "trying to catch up."
It's not about perfection—it's about building basic self-support.

• • • •

Cleanliness: Your Environment Is a Mirror of Your Mind

HERE'S THE TRUTH:

A messy space creates a messy mind. A clean space creates a clean mind.

This doesn't mean your home needs to look like a showroom. It means your environment should support you, not drain you.

When your space is:
Cluttered
Chaotic
Dusty
Disorganized
Smelly
Neglected...your brain feels:
Overwhelmed
Stressed
Unfocused
Depressed
Unmotivated
But when your space is:

Tidy
Functional
Organized
Fresh
Comfortable…your brain feels:
Calmer
Clearer
More capable
Ready to act

Cleaning isn't about chores—it's about building a life you can breathe in.

• • • •

Laundry: It's Not About Clothes—It's About Preparedness

LAUNDRY FEELS BORING…until you don't have clean clothes and suddenly your whole day is harder.

When your clothes are:
Clean
Folded
Ready
You feel:
Put together
Presentable
Prepared
When your clothes are:
Dirty
Piled
Wrinkled
Questionable
You feel:
Behind

Scattered
Stressed
Keeping up with laundry is one of the simplest ways to prevent chaos.
It keeps you from scrambling.
It keeps you from embarrassment.
It keeps you from choosing outfits based on "what's not gross."
It's dignity in fabric form.

• • • •

Hygiene: Confidence Starts With How You Care for Your Body

PERSONAL HYGIENE IS not superficial—it's foundational. When you take care of your body, you feel more confident, more comfortable in your skin, and more grounded.
Clean teeth.
Clean body.
Clean hair.
Clean clothes.
Basic grooming.
These aren't beauty standards—**they're self-respect rituals.**
Bad hygiene creates:
Insecurity
Social anxiety
Embarrassment
Smell (and people will not tell you)
Dental problems ($$$)
Health issues ($$$)
Low self-esteem
Good hygiene creates:
Confidence
Better interactions

Physical comfort
Less anxiety
Fewer health issues
Long-term savings
It's not vanity—it's maintenance.

• • • •

Healthy Habits: Most Health Issues Come From Neglect

YOU DON'T NEED TO BE a fitness model.
You don't need to eat perfectly.
You don't need extreme routines.
You just need consistency. Because health is math:
if you neglect yourself→problems pile up
if you care for yourself→problems decrease
Neglect leads to:
Low energy
Mood swings
Chronic pain
Unnecessary medical bills
Emotional instability
Regret over what you "should have done"
Consistency leads to:
Stable mood
Better focus
Physical comfort
Higher self-esteem
Fewer emergencies
A sense of control

Healthy habits are not punishment. **They're preventative life support.**

Finances: Self-Sufficiency Builds Freedom

MONEY DOESN'T BUY HAPPINESS. But money does buy:
  Options
  Security
  Stability
  Breathing room
  Independence
When you mismanage your money, you lose all of those things. When you manage it well, you gain power.

Basic financial skills include:
  Spending only what you can afford
  Saving even small amounts
  Avoiding impulsive buys
  Planning for expenses
  Saying no when needed
  Not living in denial

This is how you avoid the trap of "I owe someone"—which often leads to:
  Dependency
  Obligation
  Guilt
  Pressure
  Compromised choices

When you can support yourself, you don't end up in situations where someone can say, "You owe me," and turn that into leverage.

Independence protects your peace.

• • • •

Self-Responsibility: The Skill That Makes Life Easier

THIS IS THE CORE OF adulthood: **Doing what needs to be done before it becomes a problem.**

Self-responsibility doesn't mean doing everything alone—it means doing your part consistently.

It keeps your life running smoothly.
It keeps stress small.
It keeps problems manageable.
It keeps you proud of yourself.

Most people think discipline is hard. But living without discipline is harder.

Cleaning up your mess in the moment? Five minutes and done. Cleaning it up after a month? An all day chore.

Paying the bill on time? Easy. Paying the late fees? Not easy.

Taking care of your health? Responsible. Fixing preventable health issues? Stressful.

Do it now and it's manageable. Do it later and it's chaos.

• • • •

Integrity: The Quiet Backbone of Your Life

INTEGRITY ISN'T ABOUT perfection.

It's about honesty.
Reliability.
Being someone you can trust.
When you live with integrity:
People respect you
Your word means something
You feel steady
You sleep easier
You avoid unnecessary drama

When you don't:
You feel guilty
You avoid people
You lose trust in yourself
You create chaos
Life gets heavier
Integrity is the simplest, fastest way to build a life that feels good from the inside.

• • • •

The Goal Is Simple: Be Able to Stand on Your Own Two Feet

SELF-SUFFICIENCY ISN'T about being rigid or rejecting help. It's about:
Being capable
Being prepared
Being dependable
Being grounded
Being proud of the way you handle your life
You don't need to be perfect. You just need to be someone you can rely on. The more you build your skills and your habits, the lighter your life becomes.
Chaos decreases.
Confidence increases.
Identity stabilizes.
Self-respect rises.
This is how you walk through life with dignity and freedom.

CHAPTER 11—Boundaries: Protecting Your Time, Energy, and Sanity

People treat boundaries like they're optional. Like they're something "nice to have if you can manage it." Like they're only for people who are confident, outspoken, or unbothered by conflict.
No.
Boundaries are not optional. They are **survival skills**. If you don't set boundaries, other people—and your own impulses—will run your life for you. This chapter is here to show you the simple, practical truth:
Boundaries don't control other people. Boundaries control access to you.

• • • •

A Boundary Is Not a Fence—It's a Filter

BOUNDARIES ARE NOT walls that shut the world out. They're filters that protect what comes in.
They keep out:
Disrespect
Overwhelm
Manipulation
Obligation
Energy drain
Guilt-driven decisions
Chaos
Unnecessary stress
And they keep in:
Peace
Stability
Clarity

Dignity
Emotional safety
Time
Energy
Self-respect
You're not shutting people out. **You're keeping yourself safe.**

• • • •

Most People Don't Lack Boundaries—They Lack Permission to Have Them

PEOPLE THINK LIKE THIS:
"I don't want to hurt their feelings."
"I don't want to seem rude."
"I don't want them to think I'm selfish."
"I don't want to disappoint anyone."
"I don't want conflict."
So instead of saying no...
You say yes.
Again.
And again.
And again.
Until suddenly your entire life is full of commitments, relationships, tasks, and responsibilities you never meant to agree to. The truth?
Saying yes to everyone else is saying no to yourself. Boundaries fix that.

• • • •

Your Time Is Finite. Your Energy Is Finite. Your Sanity Is Finite.

YOU ONLY GET SO MANY hours. So much mental capacity. So much emotional space. If you don't protect them, they get taken.
People aren't evil—they're just focused on their own needs.
If you're available, they'll use your availability.
If you're flexible, they'll bend your flexibility.
If you're forgiving, they'll rely on your forgiveness.
People treat you according to what you allow. Boundaries teach people how to treat you.

• • • •

Boundaries Prevent Resentment

RESENTMENT DOESN'T come from giving. It comes from over-giving.
From:
Saying yes when you meant no
Letting people interrupt your time
Letting people drain your energy
Letting people cross lines
Letting people dictate your feelings
letting people assume access they haven't earned
Then you end up resentful—not because you're a bad person, but because you're an unprotected one. Boundaries don't make you unkind. **They make you honest.**

• • • •

Good Boundaries Sound Simple

THEY DON'T NEED DRAMA.

They don't need speeches.
They don't need justifications.
Good boundaries sound like:
"No, thank you."
"I'm unavailable."
"I can't do that today."
"That doesn't work for me."
"I'm not discussing that."
"I have plans."
"I need space."
Short. Clear. Calm. Complete.
And here's the best part: **You don't owe an explanation.**

• • • •

Boundaries Aren't About Controlling Others — They're About Controlling You

YOU CAN'T FORCE ANYONE to behave.
You can't force anyone to respect you.
You can't force anyone to change.
You can't force anyone to do the right thing.
But you can control:
Who gets your time
Who gets your energy
Who gets your emotional access
Who gets a place in your life
Who gets to stay
Who gets distance
That's what boundaries are for. Not controlling them—**containing you.**

• • • •

People Who Used To Benefit From Your Lack of Boundaries Will Resist Your Boundaries

WHEN YOU START SETTING boundaries, two things happen:
Healthy people respect them.
Unhealthy people complain.
Don't confuse someone's discomfort with your boundaries as a sign you're doing something wrong. Their reaction reveals their relationship to your wellbeing. If someone gets angry because you're protecting your peace, they are the exact reason you needed a boundary.

• • • •

Your Most Important Boundary: Protect Your Peace Like It's Property

IMAGINE YOUR PEACE as a house. It has rooms, doors, locks, and windows. You don't let just anyone walk in.
You decide:
Who gets inside
How far they get
How long they stay
When they need to leave
Your peace is your property. Treat it like it has value. **Because it does.**

• • • •

Boundaries Give You Back Three Crucial Things

1. **Time**
You suddenly have hours back you didn't realize were being stolen.
2. **Energy**

You stop feeling emotionally wrung out.
3. **Self-Respect**
You stop abandoning yourself to make others comfortable.
Boundaries don't cost you freedom—they **create** it.

• • • •

The Rule Is Simple: If It Costs You Your Peace, It's Too Expensive

THIS APPLIES TO:
People
Commitments
Conversations
Opportunities
Plans
Relationships
Responsibilities
Environments
If something consistently drains your peace, the price is too high.
Boundaries lower the cost.

• • • •

Boundaries Let You Build a Life That Fits YOU

NOT A LIFE SHAPED BY:
Pressure
Guilt
Obligation
Fear
Other people's expectations
Your old patterns
Your old insecurities

A life shaped by:
Clarity
Stability
Respect
Protection
Intention
Peace

That's the life you deserve. And boundaries are how you build it.

CHAPTER 12—Relationships: Choosing People Who Add to Your Life, Not Drain It

Relationships are one of the biggest influence points in your entire life.

They can elevate you...or erode you.

Strengthen you...or drain you.

Support your peace...or disrupt it.

Build your confidence...or break it down.

And here's the truth most people never learn: Who you let into your life determines the quality of your life.

Not fate.

Not luck.

Not the universe.

Not the "vibe."

Just simple cause and effect.

• • • •

You Don't Attract People—You Allow Them

PEOPLE LOVE SAYING, "I attract toxic people." No. Toxic people approach everyone. They choose anyone who looks open. The real issue is **who you allow in**, not who you attract.

You control:

Who gets close

Who gets access

Who gets information

Who gets your time

Who gets emotional energy

Who gets your trust
Who you invest in
Your life changes when your standards change — not when other people do.

• • • •

Relationships Should Add to Your Life, Not Complicate It

HERE'S THE MOST PRACTICAL standard you'll ever learn: **If someone makes your life heavier, they are not your person.**
Healthy relationships make your life:
Easier
Calmer
Lighter
Safer
Clearer
Happier
Unhealthy relationships make your life:
Stressful
Confusing
Draining
Dramatic
Unstable
Anxious
It's not about labeling people "good" or "bad."
It's about evaluating whether their presence improves your life or damages it.

• • • •

Confusion Is a Red Flag. Clarity Is a Green Flag.

YOU SHOULD NOT NEED a detective kit, psychic abilities, or emotional calculus to understand someone's intentions.

Confusion is a consequence—and it always has a cause.

If someone:
Sends mixed signals
Hides things
Says one thing and does another
Makes you guess
Makes you anxious
Makes you overthink
Makes you feel insecure
That is **not connection**—that is chaos disguised as chemistry.
Real connection feels clear.
Clear is calm.
Calm is safe.
Safe is sustainable.

• • • •

Energy Doesn't Lie—Pay Attention to How You Feel Around Them

YOU LEARN MORE FROM how people make you feel than from what they say. Pay attention to your internal signals:

Do you feel:
Relaxed?
Understood?
Respected?
Valued?
Calm?
Seen?

Steady?
Appreciated?
Or do you feel:
Tense?
Unsure?
Anxious?
Drained?
Invisible?
Defensive?
Pressured?
Small?

Your nervous system gives cleaner feedback than your heart sometimes. Trust that.

• • • •

The Bare Minimum Should Not Feel Like a Prize

WHEN SOMEONE:
Waits overly long to text you back
Shows a little care
Gives minimal effort
Is occasionally respectful
Apologizes only after being caught
Gives basic attention
...that is not exceptional.
That is not a steal.
That is not "finally someone good."

That is **the floor**, not the ceiling. You deserve more than the bare minimum. You deserve consistency.

• • • •

Your Standards Are Not Demands—They Are Filters

YOUR STANDARDS DON'T scare the right people away. They scare the wrong people away.

Standards protect you from:
Emotional chaos
Manipulation
Dead-end relationships
Inconsistency
Disrespect
People who want access without effort

Standards attract:
Stable people
Responsible people
Honest people
Emotionally mature people
People who are good for your life
Choose according to your standards—not your loneliness.

• • • •

Relationships Should Never Cost You Your Peace

THIS IS THE LAW: IF someone consistently disrupts your peace, the cost is too high.

Relationships should come with:
Mutual respect
Clear communication
Steady effort
Emotional safety
Basic reliability
Kindness
Alignment

Boundaries
Not:
Excuses
Confusion
Disrespect
Volatility
Hot-and-cold energy
Pressure
Guilt
Manipulation

If someone makes you feel like your peace is negotiable, they're not a partner—**they're a problem.**

• • • •

Don't Try to Fix, Change, or Rescue People

YOU ARE NOT A LIFE raft.
    You are not a therapist.
    You are not responsible for someone's healing, stability, or sanity.
    You cannot:
Love someone into maturity
Support someone into responsibility
Care someone into consistency
Fix someone into readiness
Sacrifice yourself into being respected

    People change when they want to change not when you want them to. Your job is not to fix people. Your job is to choose people who don't need to be fixed to treat you right.

• • • •

Compatibility Is About Lifestyles, Not Feelings

FEELINGS MATTER—BUT they aren't enough.
Compatibility is:
Values
Maturity
Habits
Goals
Communication style
Priorities
Emotional regulation
Attraction creates connection. Compatibility creates stability. You need both.

• • • •

Let Connections End When They End

NOT EVERY PERSON OR situation is meant to stay. Letting go doesn't mean:
You failed
They failed
Something is wrong
Someone did something wrong
It means the connection served its purpose and has run its course. Staying past the expiration date is how you turn something meaningful into something painful.
Release people with dignity — yourself included.

• • • •

Healthy Love Makes You More Yourself—Not Less

THE RIGHT RELATIONSHIPS:
   expand you
   support you
   ground you
   encourage you
   bring out your strengths
   help you grow
   Unhealthy relationships shrink you. If someone makes you feel like you need to be less—less emotional, less expressive, less yourself—that's not love. **That's a warning.**

• • • •

Choose People Who Make Your Life Better

NOT HARDER.
   Not heavier.
   Not more complicated.
   Not more dramatic.
   Not more confusing.
   Better.
   People who add:
   Encouragement
   Stability
   Wisdom
   Laughter
   Loyalty
   Honesty
   Support
   Peace

These are the relationships worth keeping, the ones that help you **build a life you're proud of.**

CHAPTER 13—The Long Game: Building a Future You Can Actually Look Forward To

Most people live like the future is some distant, optional thing. Something they'll "figure out later." Something that magically works out when they need it to. But here's the real math:

Your future is being built right now—with every choice you make.

Not someday.

Not after you "get your life together."

Not when the timing is perfect.

Right. Now.

The future isn't waiting for you to be ready.

The future is shaped by what you're doing today.

• • • •

Your Future Isn't a Mystery—It's a Trajectory

PEOPLE ACT LIKE THEIR future is unpredictable, unclear, or up to fate. It's not. Your future follows the line created by your choices.

If you're:

Studying

Planning

Saving

Thinking ahead

Building habits

Developing skills

Protecting your peace

Your trajectory is upward.

If you're:
Avoiding responsibility
Reacting instead of choosing
Chasing shiny objects
Ignoring red flags
Living in chaos
Depending on luck
Your trajectory is downward or stagnant. Not as punishment—simply as direction.

• • • •

Everything You Do Today Either Makes Tomorrow Easier or Harder

THIS IS ONE OF THE clearest cause-and-effect rules in life.
Actions accumulate.
Consequences accumulate.
Habits accumulate.
Skills accumulate.
Relationships accumulate.
It's all compounding.
Good choices compound into stability.
Bad choices compound into regret.
Most people underestimate the power of small decisions. **Small decisions are the building blocks of big futures.**

• • • •

Your Future Success Comes From Boring Consistency, Not Big Moments

PEOPLE WAIT FOR:

Motivation
Inspiration
The "perfect time"
A sign
A big break
Everything to feel right
But life doesn't change in grand events.
Life changes in:
Brushing your teeth
Cleaning your room
Sending the email
Showing up
Saying no
Saving $20
Thinking ahead
Taking care of yourself
Building habits
Choosing peace over chaos
Small things, done consistently, build massive futures.

• • • •

Thinking Long-Term Makes Short-Term Pressure Shrink

MOST BAD CHOICES COME from short-term thinking:
"I just want to feel better."
"I don't want to miss out."
"I need X now."
"I don't have another choice."
"I'll deal with it tomorrow."
Long-term thinking changes the equation.
The moment you think about future-you
The one who has to live with the outcome

The shiny object loses its shine.
Future-you becomes part of the decision. That's maturity in action.

• • • •

Your Future Self Is Counting on You

PICTURE YOURSELF FIVE years from now.
Does that version of you:
Feel stable?
Feel proud?
Feel secure?
Feel healthy?
Feel calm?
Feel respected?
Feel financially steady?
Feel happy?
Feel confident?
Feel at peace?
Or does that version feel:
Tired?
Overwhelmed?
Unstable?
Behind?
Stressed?
Regretful?
Anxious?
Trapped?
That version of you depends on your choices. Your future self is **your responsibility**.
Every choice either: builds you up or breaks you down.

• • • •

Play the Long Game With Everything That Matters

RELATIONSHIPS
Choose people who support your future, not just your present.
Health
Small habits today prevent big problems later.
Finance
Saving a little now prevents panic later.
Skills
Learn practical skills now so future-you doesn't struggle.
Reputation
The way you treat others becomes the way you are remembered.
Peace
Protect your emotional stability like it's your retirement plan—because it is.

• • • •

Short-Term Thinking Creates Long-Term Problems

AVOIDING DISCOMFORT today creates chaos tomorrow.
Avoiding responsibility today: Bigger issues later.
Ignoring red flags today: Harder heartbreak later.
Spending impulsively today: Money stress later.
Dating someone chaotic today: Emotional recovery later.
Skipping self-care today: Health problems later.
Talking too much today: Consequences later.
Short-term comfort creates long-term cost.
Long-term thinking protects your future.

• • • •

THE CAUSE AND EFFECT SURVIVAL GUIDE

Long-Term Thinking Doesn't Steal Fun—It Prevents Regret

A COMMON MISUNDERSTANDING: People think thinking ahead ruins spontaneity.
No.
It prevents regret.
It prevents chaos.
It prevents guilt.
It prevents consequences you didn't need to experience.
Long-term thinking doesn't remove fun—it **removes** damage. Fun becomes fun again when it doesn't come with pain attached.

• • • •

Your Future Is Built on One Simple Question

EVERY CHOICE FILTERS down to this: **"What will this return to my life later?"**
Not "What do I want right now?"
Not "What feels good?"
Not "What is everyone else doing?"
Not "What can I get away with?"
What will this do to me?
If people learned that question at age 14...there would be a lot fewer adults drowning in regret.

• • • •

The Long Game Is the Freedom Game

THINKING LONG-TERM gives you:
Stability
Confidence

Emotional safety
Financial safety
The ability to say no
The ability to walk away
Choices that pay off
Opportunities that last
Relationships that work
Peace that stays
It is not restrictive. **It is liberating.**

When you work toward building a future you can trust...the present becomes a place you can actually enjoy.

CHAPTER 14—Self-Respect: The Compass That Makes Every Choice Easier

If you want to simplify your entire life—your choices, your relationships, your habits, your boundaries, your confidence—you don't need a hundred rules.

You need **self-respect**.

Self-respect is the internal voice that says:

"I matter."

"My peace matters."

"My time matters."

"My standards matter."

"My future matters."

"My wellbeing matters."

And once that belief sits in the center of your identity, everything else becomes easier.

Not perfect.

Not effortless.

But easier.

Because self-respect becomes the compass that points you toward the right choices and away from the wrong ones.

• • • •

Self-Respect Is Built, Not Bought

YOU DON'T GET SELF-respect by:

    Saying affirmations

    Being confident

    Getting validation

    Looking good

    Being successful

Being liked
Having attention

Self-respect doesn't come from outside. It comes from **what you do for yourself**. You earn it. Each good choice you make in your own favor—every time you walk away, pause, think ahead, protect your peace, or hold a boundary—self-respect grows a little bit.

It's not magic.
It's accumulation.

• • • •

Self-Respect Is the Opposite of Self-Abandonment

HERE'S THE TRUTH:

Every time you go against yourself you chip away at your self-respect.

Action: You say yes when you want to say no.
Return: You feel small and resentful.
Action: You tolerate disrespect.
Return: You question your own worth.
Action: You ignore red flags.
Return: You pay the emotional price later.
Action: You choose short-term comfort over long-term peace.
Return: You deal with regret and stress.

Self-respect doesn't disappear overnight. It erodes choice by choice. And it rebuilds the same way.

• • • •

Your Choices Teach You How to See Yourself

THIS IS VITAL: YOU learn your worth by how you treat yourself.
If you keep your promises to yourself, you see yourself as reliable.

If you protect your energy, you see yourself as valuable.
If you make responsible choices, you see yourself as capable.
If you avoid drama, you see yourself as grounded.
If you walk away from chaos, you see yourself as strong.
If you speak calmly and intentionally, you see yourself as mature.

• • • •

Every choice sends a message: "This is the kind of person I am." And those messages add up to self-respect.

SELF-RESPECT MAKES Saying No Easy.
When you don't respect yourself, "no" feels mean or selfish. When you do respect yourself, "no" feels obvious.
Self-respect creates clarity:
"I'm not available for that."
"That doesn't work for me."
"That's not my responsibility."
"That's not aligned with the life I'm building."
Self-respect isn't loud. It's not dramatic. It's not defensive. **It's steady.**

• • • •

Self-Respect Makes You Immune to Manipulation

MANIPULATION THRIVES when someone doubts their own value. But if you respect yourself, it's much harder for someone to:
Guilt-trip you
Pressure you
Shame you
Take advantage of you
Override your boundaries

Convince you to settle
Lure you into chaos

Self-respect keeps your emotional doors locked to people who don't treat you well. It's not that you can't be fooled—you can. It's that you recover very quickly because your standards kick back in.

• • • •

Self-Respect Stabilizes Your Emotions

SELF-RESPECT CREATES:
    Less anxiety
    Less overthinking
    Fewer regrets
    Less self-doubt
    More confidence
    More calm
    More trust in yourself
It stabilizes you internally:
Because you stop negotiating with yourself.
You stop abandoning yourself.
You stop making choices that hurt you.
You stop tolerating situations that drain you.

And your internal world becomes a safer place. And when your inner world is stable, the outer world becomes easier to navigate.

• • • •

Self-Respect Makes the Long Game Feel Natural

WHEN YOU RESPECT YOURSELF, long-term thinking stops feeling like sacrifice. It feels like protection.

You naturally choose:

Better relationships
Better habits
Better environments
Better opportunities
Better boundaries
Better conversations
Better priorities

Because you finally understand that your future matters. Self-respect aligns your choices with the life you want—not the life you want to escape from.

• • • •

Self-Respect Doesn't Make You Harsh—It Makes You Whole

SOME PEOPLE CONFUSE self-respect with arrogance or coldness. No.

Self-respect isn't:
Rude
Defensive
Selfish
Superior
Dismissive
Controlling

Self-respect is:
Clear
Calm
Grounded
Stable
Honest
Mature
Protective

You're not shutting others out. You're refusing to shut yourself out.

Your Self-Respect Sets the Tone for Your Entire Life

YOUR RELATIONSHIPS improve.
    Your decisions improve.
    Your habits improve.
    Your environment improves.
    Your health improves.
    Your boundaries improve.
    Your sense of peace improves.
    Your self-esteem improves.
    Self-respect is the root. Everything else grows from it.

CHAPTER 15—Your Environment: The Hidden Force Shaping You Every Day

People think their personality, motivation, discipline, and confidence come from inside.

But the truth is simpler—and far more practical:

Your environment is shaping you just as much as your choices are.

Not just the big things.

The subtle things.

The everyday things.

The things you barely notice because you're so used to them.

Your environment can support your peace...or sabotage it.

It can lift you up...or gradually pull you down.

• • • •

Your Environment Affects You Even When You're Not Paying Attention

YOUR BRAIN IS CONSTANTLY scanning the space around you.

Messy room?

Your brain registers it.

Chaotic household?

Your emotions absorb it.

Negative people?

Your energy takes the hit.

Loud, unpredictable surroundings?

Your nervous system stays tense.

Cluttered desk?

Your focus drops.

A clean, calm space doesn't magically fix your problems—but it makes your life easier to handle.

A chaotic space doesn't ruin your life—but it makes everything harder.

Your environment amplifies your emotions.

• • • •

Your Environment Shapes Your Mood, Motivation, and Mental Health

WHAT YOU SEE EVERY day becomes your baseline. If your environment is chaotic, you become reactive. If your environment is calm, you become grounded.

This isn't psychology. **It's cause and effect.**

A messy room creates:
Low motivation
Brain fog
Distraction
Stress
Shame
Procrastination

A tidy room creates:
Clarity
Readiness
Calm
Confidence
Intention

You don't need perfection. You need order. Order supports you.
Chaos drains you.

• • • •

You Absorb the Energy of the People Around You

YOUR ENVIRONMENT ISN'T just the physical space—it's the emotional space too.

If the people around you are:
Dramatic
Negative
Lazy
Impulsive
Disrespectful
Chaotic
Inconsistent
Constantly complaining
Gossiping
Fighting

You absorb the atmosphere.

Not because you're weak—but because humans are naturally influenced by their surroundings.

You become what you're around.

Put yourself in a room full of miserable people, and your mood will sink. Put yourself in a room full of motivated people, and you'll rise.

Energy is contagious. Make sure you're catching the right kind.

• • • •

Your Environment Shapes Your Standards

IF EVERYONE AROUND you:
Settles
Tolerates disrespect
Makes reckless choices
Blames others
Avoids responsibility

Stays in chaos
Lives in denial
Their standard becomes the norm—and you naturally lower yours to match.

But if the people around you:
Work on themselves
Take responsibility
Think ahead
Maintain their space
Protect their peace
Practice boundaries
Respect their time
Make intentional choices

Your standards rise effortlessly. Your environment either elevates you or erodes you. There is no neutral.

• • • •

Your Environment Can Quietly Ruin Your Progress

YOU CAN BE DOING ALL the right things:
Learning
Trying
Improving
Healing
Growing

But if your environment contradicts your effort, it pulls you backward.

If you are:
Trying to study in chaos→**you lose focus.**
Trying to be calm around loud, volatile people→**you stay tense.**
Trying to save money while surrounded by impulsive spenders→**you cave.**

THE CAUSE AND EFFECT SURVIVAL GUIDE

Trying to stay peaceful while surrounded by drama→you get **sucked in**.

Trying to make good choices while surrounded by reckless people→ **you slide**.

Not because you're weak—but because environment always influences behavior.

You can't out-discipline a destructive environment.

• • • •

Your Environment Should Match the Life You're Trying to Build

ASK YOURSELF: DOES my environment support my goals or sabotage them?

If you want:
Peace→your space must be calm
Discipline→your space must be ordered
Self-respect→your space must reflect care
Focus→your space must be clean
Emotional safety→your circle must be stable
Better choices→your surroundings must not tempt chaos
Create the conditions that support the best version of you.
You don't need a fancy house.
You need a structured one.
You need a respectful one.
You need a calm one.

• • • •

Sometimes You Need to Change Your Environment to Change Your Life

YOU CAN CHANGE YOURSELF.

You can change your habits.
You can change your mindset.
But sometimes...
You need to:
Clean your room
Change who you hang out with
Adjust your routine
Organize your life
Close the door to certain people
Stop letting others' chaos leak into your environment
Give yourself a space that feels safe
This doesn't have to be dramatic. Small changes create big shifts.
A cleaner space.
Different friends.
Better routines.
More silence.
Less noise.
More structure.
Your environment should lift you, not drain you.

· · · ·

Your Space Reflects How You Treat Yourself

A NEGLECTED ENVIRONMENT is a sign of self-neglect.
    A cared-for environment is a sign of self-respect.
    When you take care of your space, you send yourself a message:
"I deserve calm."
"I deserve order."
"I deserve comfort."
"I deserve a life that supports me."
    The space you live in becomes the space you think in. Curate it with intention.

• • • •

Your Environment Is One of the Easiest Things to Improve—and the Most Impactful

YOU CAN'T ALWAYS CHANGE:
  Your past
  Your parents
  Your circumstances
  Your genetics
  Your opportunities

But you can change your environment. And when you do, your mental health, choices, mood, habits, and progress all improve automatically.

Because environment is the silent architect of your life.

CHAPTER 16—Goals & Direction: How to Move Forward Without Overwhelm

Most people fail not because they're lazy, unmotivated, or incapable—but because they're trying to do everything at once. Life feels overwhelming when you're staring at the entire mountain.

The truth is simple:

You don't climb a mountain in one step, you climb it in thousands of small, boring, consistent ones.

In this chapter, we're not talking about big, dramatic dreams. We're talking about direction—the everyday momentum that moves your life somewhere better.

• • • •

You Don't Need a Perfect Plan—You Need a Starting Point

PEOPLE STALL THEIR entire lives waiting for:
- the right moment
- the right mood
- the right plan
- the right motivation
- the right partner
- the right environment
- the right energy

But progress doesn't come from readiness.

Progress comes from starting.

Even if your start is small.
Even if it's messy.
Even if you don't feel confident.
Starting creates clarity.
Starting creates direction.

Starting creates momentum.
Waiting creates nothing.

• • • •

Small Steps Change Your Life More Than Big Intentions

BIG INTENTIONS FEEL good. They make you feel like you're doing something just by thinking about them.

But nothing changes until you take action—tiny action.

Small steps:

Build discipline

Reduce overwhelm

Keep you moving

Build identity

Prevent backslides

Create momentum

Stack into progress

People want transformation without the tiny steps that create it.

But those steps are the transformation.

• • • •

Direction Beats Speed Every Time

YOU DON'T NEED TO MOVE fast—you need to move in the right direction.

People rush into things:

Fad diets

Impulsive plans

Unrealistic goals

Huge commitments

Sudden changes

Then they burn out and think they failed. You didn't fail—you sprinted when the goal was a marathon.

Progress is slow by design.
Slow is sustainable.
Slow is stable.
Slow gets you there.
Speed gets you overwhelmed.

• • • •

Overwhelm Comes From Trying to Live the Whole Future at Once

THE FUTURE CAN BE PARALYZING if you try to carry all of it today.

You don't need to:
Be perfect
Know everything
Map everything
Fix everything
Handle everything at once

You just need to do the next right thing. Not the next hundred right things. Just one. Then another. Then another. That's how people change their lives.

• • • •

Your Goals Need to Be Realistic, Not Romantic

ROMANTIC GOALS SOUND like this:
"I'm going to change everything overnight."
"I'll wake up at 5 AM and change my entire routine."
"I'll save half my paycheck starting tomorrow."
"I'll fix my whole life this week."

Beautiful on paper. Impossible in practice.
Realistic goals sound like this:
"I'll drink more water this week."
"I'll clean one area of my room today."
"I'll save $10."
"I'll leave five minutes earlier."
"I'll do five minutes of reading."
"I'll respond thoughtfully instead of impulsively."
Small goals don't feel magical—but they create real change.
Romantic goals feel magical—but they collapse under pressure.

· · · ·

Your Direction Should Match the Life You Want, Not the Life You're Used To

THIS PART IS KEY:
Don't choose your goals based on who you've been. Choose them based on who you want to become.
If you want:
Stability→choose habits that create stability
Confidence→choose habits that build self-respect
Health→choose habits that support your body
Peace→choose habits that protect your time and energy
Better relationships→choose habits that support boundaries and clarity
Your goals should be aligned with the future you're walking into—not the past you're trying to outgrow.

· · · ·

Consistency Matters More Than Intensity

A LITTLE EVERY DAY beats a lot once in a while.
Consistency:
Rewires your brain
Changes your habits
Strengthens your identity
Builds competence
Builds trust in yourself
Intensity creates burnout. Consistency creates capability.
Five minutes a day is better than two hours once a week.
Because consistency is who you **become**. Intensity is something you try.

• • • •

You Don't Have to See the Whole Path—Just the Next Step

YOUR BRAIN LOVES CERTAINTY. It wants to know everything before doing anything.
But that's not how life works. You gain clarity by moving, not by thinking. Every step you take reveals the next one.
It's like walking with a flashlight: You only see a few feet ahead, but that's all you need to keep going.
You don't need the full map. Just the next marker.

• • • •

Progress Is Not Linear—It's Directional

YOU WILL:
Have bad days
Fall behind

Lose motivation
Slip back into old habits
Get tired
Get distracted
That's normal.
Progress is not a straight line—it's a general direction.
The question is never, "Did you mess up?"
The question is, "Did you get back on track?"
If you get back on track, you're winning.

• • • •

Goals Are Not Pressure—They're Guidance

GOALS ARE NOT THERE to:
Shame you
Pressure you
Overwhelm you
Stress you
They're there to guide you:
This way, not that way
Forward, not sideways
Intentional, not chaotic
Stable, not reactive
Goals are a compass, not a courtroom.

• • • •

The Right Goals Build a Future That Feels Like You

NOT A FUTURE FORCED by external pressure.
Not a future shaped by fear.
Not a future chosen for approval.

Not a future that looks good but feels wrong.
A future that matches:
Your values
Your peace
Your personality
Your pace
Your needs
Your dreams
Your standards
A future you actually want to live in—not escape from.

CHAPTER 17—Consequences: The Honest Math of Cause and Effect (Where Most People Go Wrong)

Most people talk about consequences like they're **punishments.**

Something the universe hands out when you've "done something bad."

Something random.

Something unfair.

Something you don't deserve.

But consequences aren't punishments. **Consequences are math.** They are the predictable return of your actions.

Every choice returns something.

Some returns are good.

Some are harmful.

Some cost you a little.

Some cost you everything.

The problem is not that people don't know consequences exist—it's that they don't think consequences apply to them.

Let's look at the math.

• • • •

Consequences Are Not Personal—They're Automatic

THE UNIVERSE IS NOT singling you out. Your life is not cursed. You're not "unlucky." Consequences simply follow actions the way shadows follow light.

Action→Return

Cause→Effect

Behavior→Outcome
Choice→Result

If you touch a hot stove, you get burned. Not because you're bad—because that's how heat works. If you ignore a responsibility, a problem grows. Not because the world hates you—but because that's how neglect works.

Consequences don't judge you. They just follow you.

• • • •

Most People Complain About Consequences While Continuing the Behavior

THIS IS THE MOST HONEST part of adulthood: People want different outcomes without different actions.

They want:
Peace, but choose drama
Trust, but lie
Stability, but avoid responsibility
Good relationships, but ignore red flags
Confidence, but abandon themselves
Money, but spend impulsively
Respect, but tolerate disrespect
Progress, but avoid effort
Health, but neglect their body
Happiness, but choose short-term relief

Then they're shocked at the return. But consequences aren't random—they're earned. Not as punishment—but as math.

• • • •

You Don't Get to Choose the Consequence—Only the Action

PEOPLE THINK THEY CAN "manage" the outcome, that they can take the action but avoid the cost. That's not how it works.

You can:
Ignore the homework, but not the failing grade
Ghost someone, but not avoid the reputation
Cheat, but not avoid the mistrust
Procrastinate, but not avoid the stress
Overspend, but not avoid the financial strain
Avoid boundaries, but not avoid resentment
Indulge impulses, but not avoid regret

The action is the only part you control. The consequence is already attached.

• • • •

Bad Choices Don't Ruin Your Life—Repeated Bad Choices Do

ONE MISTAKE IS HUMAN. Two mistakes is a pattern. Three mistakes is a trajectory.

Bad decisions only become life-changing when they become habits.
One bad relationship? You learn.
Five bad relationships? You're choosing the same red flags.
One impulsive spend? Whatever.
Chronic impulsive spending? You're in financial panic.
One night of chaos? Okay.
A lifestyle of chaos? Your life becomes unlivable.
Consequences compound—just like good choices do.

• • • •

There Are Immediate Consequences and Delayed Consequences

IMMEDIATE CONSEQUENCES teach quickly.

You snap at someone→they snap back.
You eat something awful→you feel sick.
You stay up too late→you're exhausted.

But delayed consequences are where most people get confused. Because nothing "bad" happens at first.

Skip brushing your teeth→nothing happens...yet.
Skip cleaning→nothing happens...yet.
Stay in a toxic relationship→nothing happens...yet.
Avoid responsibility→nothing happens...yet.

But over time...

Decay sets in.
Health declines.
Self-respect erodes.
Problems pile up.
Regret gains weight.

Delayed consequences are quiet—until they're not.

• • • •

You Always Know the Consequence If You're Honest With Yourself

PEOPLE PRETEND THEY "didn't know." But honesty reveals the truth: **You knew.**

You knew:
The relationship was wrong
The friend was shady
The habit was unhealthy
The choice was reckless
The environment was toxic

THE CAUSE AND EFFECT SURVIVAL GUIDE 107

The impulse was dangerous
The shortcut would cost you
The feeling was a warning
People don't miss red flags —they ignore them.
Consequences don't surprise you when you stop lying to yourself.

• • • •

Your Life Right Now Is the Return of Previous Choices

THIS SENTENCE STINGS—BUT it liberates you: **Your current life is the result of past choices. Your future life will be the result of current choices.**

This doesn't mean everything is your fault. It doesn't erase trauma or hardship. It means you are powerful. Because if your past choices shaped your present, then your current choices shape your future.

You can redirect your trajectory at any time.

• • • •

Consequences Are the Universe's Most Honest Teacher

CONSEQUENCES DON'T lie.
They don't sugarcoat.
They don't negotiate.
They don't argue.
They don't bend.
And unlike people they tell you the truth about your choices. Consequences won't flatter you, spare your feelings, or tell you what you want to hear. They'll reflect your behavior back to you in full clarity.

The good news? They can reflect positive behavior too.

Good Choices Have Consequences Too—Positive Ones

PEOPLE FORGET THIS part: Good choices come with returns just as predictable as bad ones.
 These returns just happen to feel better:
Saying no→peace later
Cleaning your room→clarity later
Studying→confidence later
Saving money→freedom later
Walking away from red flags→stability later
Protecting your health→strength later
Setting boundaries→healthier relationships later
Thinking ahead→smoother days later
Self-respect→better standards later
 Good choices compound into a good life. Not instantly—but predictably.

• • • •

Consequences Don't Care About Your Intent—Only Your Action

YOU CAN HAVE THE BEST intentions in the world but consequences follow behavior, not intention. You might mean well...but if your actions cause harm, the consequence arrives.
 You might not intend to ruin your day...but if you procrastinate, the stress arrives.
 You might not intend to lose someone's trust...but if you lie, the distrust arrives.
 Intention matters morally. Action matters practically. **Consequences are practical.**

When You Learn to See Consequences in Advance, You Become Unstoppable

THIS IS THE SECRET to maturity:

Being able to predict the return of your actions before you take them.

This skill makes you:
calmer
wiser
less impulsive
more stable
more successful
more respected
more in control

It gives you a massive advantage because you stop making choices you'll regret.

It's not magic, it's return.

You start thinking:

"What will this return to my life?"

"What does this action lead to?"

"Is this worth the cost?"

"Will this matter in a week? A year?"

"How do I feel after this choice?"

When you can see the consequence coming, you stop walking into fire.

CHAPTER 18—Temptation & Shiny Objects: How the World Tricks You Into Choosing Regret

If consequences are the math of life, shiny objects are the distractions that make people forget the math exists. A shiny object is anything that feels good in the moment but costs you later. It doesn't matter what the shiny object is — a person, an opportunity, a night out, a decision, a shortcut, an impulse — they all work the same way:

Short-term pleasure.
Long-term regret.

• • • •

Shiny Objects Are Designed to Distract You From Consequences

THE REASON SHINY OBJECTS are dangerous isn't because they're evil but because they're exciting.

Shiny objects give you a hit of something you think is missing from your life:

Attention
Validation
Adrenaline
Desire
Escape
Entertainment
Ego boost
Novelty

Your brain LOVES novelty—it's wired to chase it. Shiny objects promise instant gratification with zero effort. **But here's the catch**: They never show you the **cost** up front. They only show you the sparkle.

The bill shows up later—usually with interest.

• • • •

Shiny Objects Speak the Language of "Don't Lose Out"

SHINY OBJECTS WHISPER:
"You deserve this."
"Everyone else is doing it."
"You can handle the consequences."
"It's not a big deal."
"You're young."
"You're bored."
"You're stressed."
"It's just once."
"You can fix it later."
The bait and switch is subtle but has a powerful pull:
Forget about the future.
There is only this the moment.
But if you are thinking long-term you will see right through the illusion being offered and decide not to bite.

• • • •

Shiny Objects Have Predictable Categories

THERE ARE THREE MAIN types:
   1. Pleasure Traps
   These feel good immediately but backfire fast:
   Impulsive sex
   Texting your ex
   Drinking "just one" more
   Overspending

Giving in to cravings
Reckless nights
The return:
Shame, regret, chaos, consequences.
2. Validation Traps
These boost your ego but damage your life:
Attention from the wrong people
Approval from people you shouldn't care about
Saying yes so people like you
Chasing popularity
Performing for others
The return:
Identity confusion, insecurity, drama, consequences.
3. Opportunity Traps
These look like growth but actually drain you:
Too-good-to-be-true offers
Fast money
Flashy jobs with red flags
Relationships that start intense but crash hard
Projects you don't have the bandwidth for
The return:
Burnout, instability, wasted time, consequences.

Different traps. Same results-consequences you don't want to deal with but have to because you created them.

• • • •

The Bait-and-Switch Effect

THIS IS HOW SHINY OBJECTS actually work:
  Step 1: Offer pleasure
  Step 2: Cloud your judgment
  Step 3: Make consequences seem small

Step 4: Hook you with emotion
Step 5: Deliver regret
Step 6: Keep you coming back for more

They hit your nervous system with dopamine before your logic has a chance to speak.

You're not weak.

You're human.

Shiny objects manipulate your biology.

• • • •

Shiny Objects Thrive on Impulse—Pausing Kills Them

EVERY shiny object loses power the moment you pause long enough to ask:

"What is the return on this?"

"How does this end?"

"What will this bring back into my life?"

"Would future-me thank me or hate me?"

"If someone I loved was in this position, would I tell them to do it?"

Shiny objects need speed.

They need impulse.

They need emotion.

The moment you slow down they lose their shine.

• • • •

Shiny Objects Show Up Most When You're Vulnerable

IF YOU'RE:
   Bored
   Lonely

Stressed
Insecure
Overwhelmed
Tired
Craving connection
Avoiding responsibility
Wanting to escape

You are vulnerable, accessible and in an emotional state perfect for manipulation.

The world doesn't offer you shiny objects because you're strong—it offers them because you're vulnerable. **Knowing your own weak spots is how you stay safe.**

• • • •

You Must Learn to Walk Away From What You Want in the Moment to Get What You Want in Your Life

THIS IS EMOTIONAL ADULTHOOD:

Choosing your long-term wellbeing over your short-term temptation.

Not because you're disciplined.
Not because you're perfect.
Not because you're strict.

But because you know the cost. You know:
What this shiny object leads to
What this moment turns into
What this decision will return
What you're truly risking

It's not sacrifice—**it's strategic.**

• • • •

Temptation Isn't a Sign of Weakness—It's a Test of Direction

YOU WILL **ALWAYS** face shiny objects. You can't avoid them. But you can outsmart them.

Temptation simply asks:

"Which version of you is driving the bus—the impulsive one or the intentional one?"

That's it. You can feel the pull but you don't have to choose it. Strength isn't the absence of temptation. Strength is your ability to choose despite it.

• • • •

The World Is Full of Shiny Objects—But Peace Is Rare

PEACE DOESN'T SPARKLE.
    Peace doesn't shout.
    Peace doesn't tempt you.
    Peace doesn't demand attention.
    Peace is quiet.
    Stable.
    Steady.
    Predictable.
    Long-term.
    Shiny objects are loud.
    Exciting.
    Instant.
    Dramatic. Short-lived.
    Peace may not be glamorous but it does make you shine.

• • • •

Your New Rule: If the Beginning Feels Too Good, Look Twice

SHINY OBJECTS ALWAYS have dramatic beginnings.
   High intensity.
   Big promises.
   Fast emotions.
   Strong energy.
   Immediate gratification.
   But good things—real good things—start slow.
   They build.
   They stabilize.
   They grow naturally.
   They feel calm.
   Shiny objects rush you. Peace never does.

• • • •

Walking Away Feels Powerful—And It Should

THERE IS NOTHING LIKE the internal thrill of resisting a shiny object. That moment where you feel the temptation…but choose your peace instead. You hear a "Good job!" whispered within you and you grin as you feel a surge of pride because you saw the consequence ahead and saved yourself.

That's the kind of reinforcement that builds a strong, grounded, confident life.

Walking away isn't loss. **It's freedom.**

CHAPTER 19—Emotional Traps: How Your Feelings Trick You Into Bad Decisions

You can be smart, aware, and well-intentioned—and still make terrible choices if your emotions are driving the bus.
Why?
Because emotions are loud.
They overpower logic.
They distort reality.
They minimize danger.
They amplify desire.
They wave away consequences.
The problem isn't that you have emotions—you're supposed to. The problem is when you trust temporary emotions to make permanent decisions.
Let's map out the emotional traps that catch nearly everyone.

• • • •

1. The "I Just Want to Feel Better" Trap

THIS IS THE MOST COMMON trap because it hits when you're in pain.
When you're:
Lonely
Stressed
Overwhelmed
Anxious
Sad
Bored
Insecure
...your brain searches for relief—not solutions.

Relief leads to:
Texting the ex
Eating the thing
Buying the thing
Saying yes
Procrastination
Running back to chaos
Falling into temptation
Self-sabotage

"When you're hurting" is when you make the **worst** long-term choices because you're only trying to make the temporary emotion go away instead of trying to understand the root of the emotion.

Relief feels good for minutes. Consequences sometimes last forever.

• • • •

2. The "I Don't Want to Lose Them" Trap

RELATIONSHIPS HIT THIS trap hard.

Fear of loss makes people:
Ignore red flags
Tolerate disrespect
Make excuses
Stay longer than they should
Settle for less
Diminish their standards
Abandon themselves to keep someone
Imagine potential instead of see reality

You're not afraid of losing them. You're afraid of losing the feeling they give you. That's an emotional illusion—not a valid reason to stay.

• • • •

3. The "It Feels Right" Trap

YOUR FEELINGS ARE NOT always the truth.
Sometimes "right" just means:
Familiar
Intense
Comfortable
Exciting
Validating
Distracting
And sometimes "wrong" just means:
Unfamiliar
New
Challenging
Uncomfortable
Your emotions are not a compass unless you've trained them. And most people haven't. If you only follow what feels right in the moment you will slip into patterns you've been trying to escape.

• • • •

4. The Anger Trap

ANGER IS A POWERFUL emotion—and a manipulative one.
Anger convinces you to:
Speak impulsively
Hit send too quickly
Escalate fights
Make threats
Say things you regret
Take actions you can't undo
Anger makes you feel powerful because you think it will allow you to win something.

Anger overshadows your:
Values
Consequences
But **anger is short-lived.**
Consequences are not.
Never make decisions when you're angry. You're choosing from pain—not wisdom.

• • • •

5. The "I Don't Want to Disappoint Anyone" Trap

THIS ONE CATCHES PEOPLE-pleasers and kind souls.
You make decisions based on:
Avoiding guilt
Avoiding conflict
Keeping the peace
Being liked
Being agreeable
Avoiding awkwardness
But here's the math: **Avoiding disappointment today creates resentment tomorrow.**
You can't live your life by someone else's comfort. That's emotional captivity. Self-respect collapses when guilt is louder than your needs.

• • • •

6. The Anxiety Trap: The Worst-Case-Scenario Spiral

ANXIETY TRIES TO CONVINCE you the worst outcome is guaranteed.
So you:
Overthink

Overanalyze
Avoid decisions
Freeze
Choose the "safest" option
Stay small
Avoid opportunities
Avoid boundaries
Stay in familiar pain instead of unfamiliar growth

Anxiety *feels* like truth—but it's just fear in a loud costume. You can't build a better life when fear is in charge.

• • • •

7. The "I Don't Want to Miss Out" Trap (FOMO)

THIS ONE DERAILS YOUNG people constantly.

You choose:
The party
The crowd
The event
The shiny object
The impulsive decision

...because you're afraid of missing something fun. But here's the reality:

You're not missing out. You're creating the future everyone else will miss out on.

Missing one event won't change anything. Making one reckless choice might.

FOMO is a trap dressed in glitter.

• • • •

8. The "They Need Me" Trap

THIS IS HOW MANIPULATORS, unstable people, and emotional vampires get in.
They make you feel responsible for:
Their stability
Their emotions
Their safety
Their happiness
Their crises
Your compassion becomes your weakness.

Here's the truth: Someone needing you is not the same as someone being good for you.

Help people, yes. But don't lose yourself in the process.

• • • •

9. The Loneliness Trap

LONELINESS CONVINCES you to:
Settle
Lower your standards
Entertain attention that isn't good for you
Chase connection instead of compatibility
Stay where you don't belong
Respond to people you've outgrown

But the truth is this: **Loneliness is temporary. Regret is not.**

Choosing someone just because you're lonely creates the exact pain you were trying to avoid.

• • • •

10. The Nostalgia Trap

YOUR BRAIN LIES TO you about the past. It only remembers the good parts.

This trap leads you back to:
Exes
Old friendships
Old habits
Old environments
Old patterns
Not because they were healthy—but because they were **familiar**.
Nostalgia is comfortable but comfortable doesn't mean good.

• • • •

11. The Ego Trap

YOUR EGO WANTS TO:
Win
Be right
Prove a point
Not look weak
Not look foolish
Not apologize
Not back down
Not lose status

Ego makes you react. Self-respect makes you choose. If you let ego drive, you will hurt yourself trying to "win" moments you don't even care about.

• • • •

The Escape Plan: How to Beat Every Emotional Trap

ONE TOOL DEFEATS THEM all:
   Pause→Breathe→Think→Decide
   Pause interrupts emotion's control.
   A breath allows you space to acknowledges the emotion without obeying it.
   Think brings logic back online.
   Decide gives you power instead of impulse.
   This is emotional intelligence in motion. This is how you avoid self-created storms.

• • • •

Final Truth of This Chapter

YOUR FEELINGS ARE REAL—**but not always right**.
   When you stop letting emotions make decisions your future-self has to pay for, you gain the quiet power that most people never experience:
   You stop living reactively and start living intentionally.

CHAPTER 20—The Identity Shift: Becoming Someone Who Chooses Well

People think change happens when you try hard enough.
    When you get motivated enough.
When life hits you hard enough.
When the timing is perfect.
When you're finally "ready."

But lasting change doesn't come from trying—it comes from **becoming**. You don't improve your life by forcing new habits onto your old identity. You improve your life by shifting the identity itself.

• • • •

Identity Is the Quiet Engine Behind Every Choice You Make

YOUR IDENTITY IS YOUR internal story — the story you tell yourself about:
    Who you are
    What you're capable of
    What you deserve
    What kind of choices you make
    What kind of future you expect
    Your actions always match your identity. Always.

If you see yourself as:
    Inconsistent→you'll act inconsistently
    A people pleaser→you'll please people
    "Bad with money"→you'll overspend
    Undisciplined→you'll avoid responsibility
    Unworthy→you'll settle
    Chaotic→you'll choose chaos

Identity drives behavior→Behavior shapes life→Life reinforces identity.

It's a loop—until you break it.

• • • •

Your Identity Right Now Is Made of Old Choices—Not Your Potential

MOST PEOPLE THINK THEIR identity is a reflection of who they ARE. But actually?
It's a reflection of:
What you tolerated
What you survived
What you believed when you didn't know better
The habits you practiced
The people you were around
The choices you made when you weren't aware
Your identity is not your destiny. It's your history.
And you're allowed to outgrow it.

• • • •

The Identity Shift Happens When You Start Making Choices as the Person You Want to Become

THIS IS THE HEART OF the chapter:
You do not wait to feel like the new version of you. You make choices AS that version before you feel like that version exists. You can't become other than you are unless you act other than you are now. It isn't faking it-it is being it until it is who you are. **You can't take on a new identity without taking it for a spin.**
Example:

You want to be responsible?
Start choosing like a responsible person—even with tiny things.
You want to be confident?
Start choosing like someone who respects themselves.
You want to be stable?
Start choosing like someone who values peace.
You choose FIRST.
The identity grows from the choices.

• • • •

Your Brain Learns Who You Are Based on What You Do Repeatedly

YOUR BRAIN IS ALWAYS adjusting to your actions.
It pays attention to:
What you follow through on
How you treat yourself
What you tolerate
What you walk away from
What you prioritize
What you sacrifice
What you protect
What you allow
Every time you choose something good for you, your brain updates the internal file: "Oh...this is who we are now."
Identity grows from consistency, not intensity.

• • • •

Becoming Someone Who Chooses Well Doesn't Require Perfection—Just Alignment

YOU DON'T NEED:
- Perfect choices
- Perfect habits
- Perfect discipline
- Perfect days

You need alignment. Alignment means your choices match:
- Your values
- Your peace
- Your standards
- Your future
- Your self-respect

Every aligned decision strengthens the identity. Every misaligned one weakens it.

You feel the difference immediately—your body tells you.

• • • •

The More You Choose Well, the More You WANT to Choose Well

THIS IS THE MIRACLE of identity shifts:

Good choices create good feelings→good feelings reinforce the identity→the identity strengthens good choices.

Suddenly:
- Saying no feels easier
- Setting boundaries feels natural
- Walking away feels powerful
- Taking care of yourself feels right
- Thinking ahead feels automatic
- Unhealthy people feel unappealing
- Temptation feels less shiny

Red flags feel obvious
You stop forcing yourself to act well because you ARE someone who acts well.
Effort becomes identity.

• • • •

Your New Identity Doesn't Need Validation—It Needs Repetition

YOU DON'T BECOME THE new version of you because someone praises you.
You become it by acting like it until it becomes who you are.
Repetition builds identity:
Respect yourself daily
Make aligned choices daily
Protect your peace daily
Speak intentionally daily
Avoid shiny objects daily
Think ahead daily
Identity isn't created by big moments. It's created by repetition.

• • • •

Who You Were Was a Survival Version—Who You Are Becoming Is the Intentional Version

THE OLD IDENTITY WAS built to:
  Cope
  Survive
  Adapt
  Get through things
  Please others
  Stay safe

Avoid conflict
Avoid abandonment

That identity kept you *alive*. This new identity will help you **live**. You're not betraying who you were. You're honoring yourself by evolving beyond it.

• • • •

You Don't Need to Announce Your Shift—Just Live It

IDENTITY SHIFTS DON'T require:
Speeches
Explanations
Apologies
Declarations
Announcements

You don't need to tell people you've changed. They'll see it.

Through:
Your boundaries
Your silence
Your stability
Your choices
Your habits
Your standards
Your energy

People will adjust. Some will fall away. Some will rise with you. All of it is part of becoming someone who chooses well.

• • • •

The Identity Shift Is the Final Step of Maturity

WHEN YOUR IDENTITY strengthens,

you stop:
Reacting
Spiraling
Chasing validation
Settling
Repeating old patterns
Abandoning yourself
Choosing short-term relief
Living by impulse
And you start:
Choosing strategically
Acting with intention
Protecting your future
Building your peace
Honoring your standards
Respecting yourself
Living cleanly
Walking confidently
This is what adulthood **feels** like when it's done well.

CHAPTER 21—Personal Responsibility: The Power to Change Your Life Is In Your Hands

Here's the truth that most people avoid their whole lives: **Your life gets better when you get better. Your life changes when you change. Your life improves when you take responsibility.**

Not blame.
Not guilt.
Not shame.

Responsibility. Taking responsibility is not about fault—it's about power.

It means you stop giving your life away to:
Excuses
Emotions
Other people
Circumstances
Fear
Denial
Childhood wounds
Bad habits
Avoidance

Responsibility returns your power to you.

• • • •

Responsibility Is Not Blame—It's Control

PEOPLE AVOID RESPONSIBILITY because they confuse it with:
Punishment

Fault
Guilt
Shame

But responsibility doesn't point a finger at the past. **It opens a door to the future.**

Responsibility says:

"I can't change what happened, but I can change what happens next."

That's power.
That's freedom.
That's adulthood.

• • • •

You Can't Change Your Past—But You Can Change Your Pattern

YOUR CHILDHOOD?
  Not your responsibility.
  Your trauma?
  Not your fault.
  Your environment growing up?
  Not your choice.
  But your:
  Healing
  Habits
  Decisions
  Boundaries
  Relationships
  Standards
  Future
  —those are your responsibility. Not because you caused your wounds, but because you deserve a better life going forward.
  Responsibility breaks the cycle.

The Opposite of Responsibility Is Helplessness

WHEN YOU AVOID RESPONSIBILITY, you tell yourself:
 "Life is happening to me."
 "I can't change anything."
 "This is just how I am."
 "This is just how life goes."
 "It's someone else's fault."
 "I can't help it."

Helplessness feels safe because it removes accountability. **But it also removes power.**

Responsibility might feel heavier —but it comes with control. You get to steer your life instead of being dragged by it.

Excuses Protect Your Present Comfort—and Destroy Your Future

EXCUSES FEEL GOOD IN the moment because they let you off the hook.
 "I'm tired."
 "I'm stressed."
 "I'll start tomorrow."
 "I don't know how."
 "It's too hard."
 "Other people have it easier."
 "It's not my fault."

But excuses don't protect you from consequences. They just delay them until they're bigger. **Every excuse you make is a wall between you and the life you want.**

Responsibility Gives You Freedom—Not Restriction

WHEN YOU TAKE RESPONSIBILITY:
    You stop waiting
    You stop depending
    You stop hoping someone else will save you
    You stop blaming
    You stop spiraling
    You stop repeating the same mistakes
    You gain:
    Clarity
    Stability
    Direction
    Confidence
    Strategy
    Momentum
    Control
    Responsibility doesn't trap you —**it liberates you.**

• • • •

Responsibility Makes Your Life Predictable—In a Good Way

WHEN YOU TAKE RESPONSIBILITY for your:
    Habits
    Choices
    Reactions
    Boundaries
    Relationships
    Time
    Money

Health
Your life becomes predictable—not chaotic.
Predictable peace.
Predictable stability.
Predictable progress.
Predictable emotional safety.
Responsibility removes the rollercoaster.

• • • •

When You Take Responsibility, Your Standards Rise Automatically

YOU DON'T HAVE TO FORCE it.
You don't have to psych yourself up.
You don't have to fake confidence.
Responsibility naturally raises your standard because you finally understand:
"I get what I accept."
"I get what I tolerate."
"I get what I choose."
"I get the life I build."
Your standards rise when you realize you're the one building.

• • • •

Responsibility Quietly Changes Your Identity

WHEN YOU CONSISTENTLY choose responsibility,
you become someone who:
Handles things
Follows through
Thinks ahead

Respects themselves
Avoids chaos
Solves problems early
Doesn't crumble under pressure
Doesn't blame others
Doesn't depend on luck

It's not loud. It's not dramatic. It's steady inner strength that builds day after day.

• • • •

Taking Responsibility Does Not Mean Doing Everything Alone

THIS IS IMPORTANT:

Responsibility means you **own your choices**—not that you reject support.

You can:
Ask for help
Get guidance
Find mentors
Go to therapy
Lean on friends
Learn from others

But responsibility means you take action with the support—you don't hand your life to someone else to fix.

You are the captain. Help is the wind in your sails. **But you steer the ship.** You determine what ports you stop in and what passengers are allowed to board.

• • • •

You Can't Fix What You Won't Admit

RESPONSIBILITY BEGINS with honesty:
"This is a pattern."
"This is hurting me."
"I keep choosing this."
"I didn't handle that well."
"I avoided the truth."
"I let this go too far."
"I created some of this pain."
"I deserve better—and I need to act like it."

Honesty isn't about self-blame. It's about self-awareness. **What you acknowledge, you can change. What you deny, you repeat.**

• • • •

Responsibility Is How You Rewrite Your Future

THE MOMENT YOU TAKE responsibility, everything shifts:
You stop repeating the same mistakes.
You stop choosing chaos.
You stop abandoning yourself.
You stop ignoring red flags.
You stop giving your power away.
And you start:
Building discipline
Protecting your peace
Choosing with intention
Walking away from what hurts you
Designing a life instead of surviving one.

Responsibility is the doorway to the life you want. Walk through it.

CHAPTER 22—Stability: Building a Life That Doesn't Fall Apart When Things Get Hard

Life will always have hard moments. Stress, disappointment, heartbreak, frustration, mistakes, unexpected events—they're all part of being human. Stability isn't about avoiding hard things. It's about being able to stay standing when they arrive.

Most people think stability comes from:
Luck
Money
Relationships
Motivation
Personality
Circumstances

But real stability comes from something much simpler: **Daily choices that make your life solid, steady, and harder to knock over.**

• • • •

Stability Is Not a Trait—It's a Structure

STABLE PEOPLE DON'T have superpowers. They have systems.
They have:
Habits
Routines
Plans
Boundaries
Standards
Responsibilities
Awareness

Discipline
None of these are glamorous. But together they create the structure that keeps you grounded.
Stability is built—not inherited.

• • • •

Stability Comes From Consistency, Not Intensity

MOST PEOPLE TRY TO "get stable" in one dramatic burst:
Clean the whole house
Overhaul their whole life
Start 10 habits at once
Make huge promises
Create extreme routines
Then they burn out—and think stability "isn't for them." No.
Stability is small.
Stability is simple.
Stability is slow.
Stability is steady.
It comes from tiny, repeatable actions done daily:
washing a dish immediately
putting things back where they belong
checking your bank account
saying no when you're overwhelmed
keeping your space in order
showing up for commitments
thinking ahead
communicating clearly
Not glamorous but **very effective.**

• • • •

THE CAUSE AND EFFECT SURVIVAL GUIDE 141

Your Environment + Your Habits = Your Stability

YOUR STABILITY IS BUILT on two foundations:
   1. Your Environment
   Is your space calm or chaotic?
   Is your circle stable or dramatic?
   Are you surrounded by support or noise?
   Your environment influences your mental state.
   2. Your Habits
   Do you follow through?
   Do you take care of yourself?
   Do you maintain order?
   Do you think ahead?
   Do you keep your word?
   Your habits influence your identity. Your environment holds you. Your habits steer you. Together, they create stability.

• • • •

Stability Means You Don't Let Problems Grow Legs

A STABLE PERSON DOESN'T avoid problems—they handle them early.
   They:
   Pay bills on time
   Respond before things pile up
   Fix small issues before they get large
   Clean messes as they go
   Speak up before resentment grows
   Address discomfort before it becomes chaos
   Think ahead before disaster strikes
   Stability is simply solving today's problems today instead of letting them become tomorrow's emergencies.

Stability Makes You Predictable—In the Best Possible Way

STABLE PEOPLE ARE CONSISTENT:
They show up.
They mean what they say.
They don't swing wildly between extremes.
They don't create unnecessary drama.
Their "no" means no.
Their "yes" means yes.
Their mood isn't a roller coaster.
Their reactions are steady.
Their life is built, not improvised.

People trust stable people—not because they're perfect, **but because they're reliable.**

• • • •

Stability Doesn't Eliminate Emotions—It Grounds Them

EMOTIONS DON'T STOP just because you build stability.
You'll still feel:
Anxious
Hurt
Angry
Sad
Overwhelmed
But stability gives you:
Coping tools
Emotional space
Self-control
Perspective

Mental clarity
Resilience
The ability to pause before reacting
Instead of being consumed by emotion, you are supported by structure. That's the difference between falling apart and bending without breaking.

• • • •

Stability Makes Your Life More Predictable, Which Makes You Feel Safer

A STABLE LIFE IS NOT boring. It's peaceful.
It feels like:
Knowing what needs to be done
Knowing how you'll handle things
Trusting yourself to make good choices
Having routines that support you
Avoiding unnecessary chaos
Staying grounded in hard moments
Stability creates internal safety—and internal safety creates confidence.

• • • •

Stability Is Built on Boring Skills That Make Life Easier

HERE ARE THE UNGLAMOROUS skills stability requires:
Cleaning
Budgeting
Planning
Pausing
Saying no

Following through
Time management
Emotional regulation
Setting boundaries
Organizing
Preparing
Choosing long-term over short-term
Protecting your environment
Making responsible decisions
These skills don't get applause but they build peace.

• • • •

Stability Makes It Easier to Recover When Life Hits Hard

A STABLE PERSON STILL falls—they just recover faster. Why?

Because they have a solid base. They don't spiral into chaos when one thing goes wrong. Their life doesn't collapse like a house of cards.

Stability cushions impact.

It turns a crisis into a problem.

A problem into an inconvenience.

An inconvenience into something manageable.

Stability doesn't make you immune to difficulty—it makes you **resilient**.

• • • •

Stability Comes From Self-Respect, Not Perfection

YOU DON'T BUILD STABILITY by being flawless. You build it by caring about the kind of life you want.

When you respect yourself:

You clean up after yourself

You handle responsibilities
You avoid chaos
You protect your peace
You think ahead
You stay intentional

Stability is a demonstration of self-respect. It says, "I care about my future so I take care of the present."

• • • •

Stability Is the Foundation of Freedom

WITHOUT STABILITY, life feels:
Reactive
Unpredictable
Chaotic
Stressful
Overwhelming
Exhausting

With stability, life feels:
Calm
Steady
Simple
Manageable
Peaceful
Empowered

Stability doesn't limit your freedom—it creates it. Because when your life is solid, you can dream bigger, choose better, and rise higher.

CHAPTER 23—Consistency: The Habit That Changes Everything (Even When You Don't Want To)

Everyone wants a better life. Few people want the process that creates it. Because the process isn't glamorous.

It's not exciting.

It's not dramatic.

It's not inspiring every day.

The process is consistency—tiny repeated actions that slowly reshape your life.

Consistency is the quiet force behind:

Confidence

Stability

Self-respect

Progress

Success

Emotional regulation

Healthy habits

Maturity

Good decision-making

• • • •

Consistency Is Boring—And That's Why It Works

YOU DON'T NEED:

Motivation

Inspiration

Perfect timing

Big energy

A new planner
A burst of confidence
Someone cheering you on
You need to repeat small actions on ordinary days. The world teaches you to chase big moments. But your life is built by small ones. Consistency is boring. But boring builds beautiful things.

• • • •

Consistency Creates Identity More Than Willpower Ever Will

WILLPOWER TRIES TO force change. Consistency becomes change.

When you consistently:
Clean a little
Think ahead
Stay calm
Follow through
Protect your peace
Maintain order
Save a bit
Organize your space
Make mature choices

Your brain starts updating your identity: "Oh... this is who we are now." **Consistency teaches your brain what kind of person you are.**

• • • •

Consistency Makes Hard Things Easy Over Time

EVERYTHING IS HARD at the beginning.
But consistency turns:
Chaos into routine

Effort into habit
Discomfort into normal
Discipline into identity
You don't need to love the task. You just need to repeat it long enough that it becomes easier. **Consistency lowers the difficulty level of life.**

• • • •

Inconsistency Is Why Most People Stay Stuck

THEY DON'T FAIL BECAUSE they're incapable—they fail because they restart constantly. Start→stop→start→stop→spiral→restart. Inconsistency erases progress.

Even tiny efforts done **inconsistently lead to**:
Frustration
Overwhelm
Loss of confidence
Self-doubt
Negative identity
Regret
Inconsistency keeps you walking around in circles going nowhere.

• • • •

Consistency Doesn't Mean Doing a Lot—It Means Doing a Little, Every Time

PEOPLE THINK CONSISTENCY means intensity. Wrong.
Consistency is:
Brushing your teeth daily
Taking 5 minutes to clean
Replying to one message

Saving $5
Walking for 10 minutes
Reading one page
Pausing before reacting
Doing the next right thing

Consistency stacked over time becomes power. Intensity stacked over time becomes burnout.

• • • •

Your Brain Loves Patterns—Use That to Your Advantage

YOUR BRAIN DOESN'T care if a habit is good or bad—it will repeat whatever you repeatedly do.

If you:
Stay up too late
Avoid tasks
Overspend
Indulge impulses
Stay in chaos
Your brain locks those in.

But if you:
Wake up at the same time
Clean your space
Think ahead
Say no
Take responsibility
Stay calm
Your brain **locks** those in. Consistency rewires you.

• • • •

Consistency Builds Self-Trust

EVERY TIME YOU FOLLOW through—even slightly—
you send yourself a message:
"I honor myself."
"I do what I say."
"I take care of myself."
"I make good choices."
"I am someone who follows through."
Self-trust is one of the most powerful forms of confidence.
Inconsistency destroys it. Consistency builds it.

• • • •

The Key to Consistency: Lower the Bar

MOST PEOPLE MAKE THE bar too high:
"I'll change everything starting tomorrow"
"I'll do a full routine every day"
"I'll make massive progress fast"
That's not realistic. It's a recipe for failure.
Consistency thrives when the bar is low, such as:
1 minute of effort
One small task
A simple routine
A tiny improvement
A single kept promise
Lower the bar to something you can ALWAYS do—then build from there.

• • • •

Consistency Doesn't Punish You for Slipping—It Welcomes You Back

LOSING CONSISTENCY isn't failure. Not returning is.

If you:
Fall off
Miss a day
Have a bad week
Lose focus
Break a routine
Get overwhelmed
Just come back. Consistency is flexible. It bends with your life. There is no "start over"—there's only **"pick up where you left off."**

• • • •

Consistency Is the Secret Behind Every "Lucky" Person You Know

PEOPLE LOVE SAYING:
"She's so lucky."
"He's gifted."
"They always get the good breaks."
No. They're consistent.

They consistently:
Protect their environment
Choose wisely
Practice good habits
Avoid drama
Manage their time
Build relationships
Think ahead
Improve themselves
Luck favors the consistent.

• • • •

Consistency Feeds Every Other Skill in This Book

IT STRENGTHENS:
- Boundaries
- Self-respect
- Stability
- Responsibility
- Emotional control
- Long-term thinking
- Good decision-making

Consistency is the multiplier—it amplifies everything else you do. Without consistency, nothing sticks. **With consistency, everything compounds.**

• • • •

Your New Identity: Someone Who Shows Up

NOT PERFECTLY.
   Not intensely.
   Not dramatically.
   But steadily.
   Daily.
   Quietly.
   Reliably.

Because people who show up—even in small ways— build the strongest, most peaceful lives.

CHAPTER 24—Self-Control: Pausing, Choosing, and Protecting Your Future

People hear "self-control" and immediately think:
Boring
Rigid
No fun
Strict
Controlling
Exhausting

But real self-control is the opposite. Self-control is freedom.
Freedom from regret.
Freedom from chaos.
Freedom from emotional whiplash.
Freedom from your own worst impulses.

Self-control isn't about limiting your life—it's about not letting short-term emotion ruin long-term peace.

• • • •

Self-Control Isn't About Willpower—It's About Awareness

MOST PEOPLE THINK SELF-control is something you force.
"Just be stronger."
"Just say no."
"Just stop doing that."
If willpower worked, you wouldn't be reading this.
Self-control begins with just one thing:
awareness of the moment you're about to sabotage yourself.
Not fixing everything.
Not being perfect.
Just noticing the moment where a bad choice is loading.

That moment is your power.

• • • •

Self-Control Lives in Five Seconds

SELF-CONTROL DOESN'T happen in hours. It happens in seconds.

The five seconds before you:
Text the ex
Overshare
Say something hurtful
Take the shiny object
Walk into chaos
Spend money you don't have
Agree to something you don't want
React impulsively
Lie to avoid conflict
Numb your feelings
Sabotage your own progress

Every bad decision has a five-second window. If you can pause during those five seconds you save yourself from the next five days, five weeks, or five years of consequences.

Self-control is a five-second power.

• • • •

Self-Control Is Pausing Long Enough for Your Future Self to Speak

YOUR PRESENT SELF WANTS:
Relief
Comfort

Validation
Distraction
Excitement
Escape
Pleasure
Your future self wants:
Peace
Stability
Dignity
Respect
Progress
Calm
Freedom

Self-control gives your future self a chance to speak up. **The pause is the bridge.**

• • • •

Impulse Is Loud. Wisdom Is Quiet.

SELF-CONTROL LETS YOU Hear the Quiet Voice.
Your impulses shout:
"Do it!"
"Who cares!"
"You deserve this!"
"It's fine!"
"Just this once!"
"You can fix it later!"
But wisdom whispers:
"Think."
"Breathe."
"This has consequences."
"You know how this ends."

"This is not worth the cost."

Without self-control, the loud voice wins. With self-control, the quiet voice gets the microphone.

• • • •

Self-Control Doesn't Remove Emotion—It Redirects It

YOU'LL STILL FEEL:
Tempted
Angry
Jealous
Lonely
Impulsive
Stressed
Overwhelmed
Reactive

Self-control doesn't erase emotion—it keeps emotion from navigating.

"You can still drive the bus you just don't get to navigate."

That's emotional maturity.

• • • •

Self-Control Protects You From You

THIS IS THE HONEST part: Most of the pain you've experienced wasn't caused by villains or fate—it was caused by moments where you abandoned yourself.

Self-control protects you from:
Your triggers
Your impulses
Your habits

Your patterns
Your emotional blind spots
Your shiny-object brain
Your old survival reactions
It saves you from the version of you that wasn't thinking clearly.
This is self-love in action.

• • • •

Self-Control Is a Skill Anyone Can Build—You Don't Need Talent

YOU DON'T HAVE TO BE born disciplined.
You don't have to be raised in structure.
You don't have to be naturally calm, organized, or patient.
Self-control is learned. You practice it like any other skill.
And here's the good news: The more you practice it, the easier it gets.
The pause grows.
The vision sharpens.
The impulse weakens.
The identity strengthens.
The future becomes clearer.
The temptation becomes smaller.
This is how people grow up emotionally—by practicing who they want to be in the moment.

• • • •

Self-Control Doesn't Restrict Your Life—It Protects Your Peace

MOST PEOPLE THINK SELF-control means living a boring life. No.
A lack of self-control is what creates:

Chaos
Regret
Drama
Shame
Self-loathing
Consequences
Guilt
Instability
Self-control creates:
Calm
Clarity
Safety
Trust
Confidence
Predictability
Self-respect
Self-control is a shield—not a cage.

• • • •

The Formula: Pause→Breathe→Think→Decide

THIS SIMPLE FOUR-STEP process can save a life:
    Pause: interrupt the impulse
    Breathe: clear the emotional fog
    Think: "What is the return? How does this end?"
    Decide: not react — decide
If you practice this formula daily, your life will radically improve.

• • • •

You Don't Need to Be Strong Forever—You Only Need to Be Strong in the Moment

PEOPLE GIVE UP ON SELF-control because they think it requires endless strength. It doesn't.

You only need strength in the moment of temptation.
In the window of impulse.
In the five seconds before regret.
Self-control is not a lifestyle—it's a moment-by-moment skill.
A pause.
A breathe.
Not a lifetime of discipline just a handful of powerful moments each day.

• • • •

Self-Control Makes You Proud of Yourself—And That Feeling Is Addictive

THERE IS NO HIGH LIKE:
    Walking away from chaos
    Resisting an impulse
    Making the smart choice
    Protecting your peace
    Choosing your future over your feelings
    Hearing the whisper of self-respect grow louder
    Hearing "dodging that bullet" from within
    Feeling yourself rise above your old patterns
That pride is intoxicating. It's the reward that replaces the impulse. You start choosing well because it **feels good** to choose well.

CHAPTER 25—Maturity: Growing Into the Version of Yourself You're Meant to Be

People think maturity comes with age. It doesn't.

You've met 50-year-olds who act like teenagers and teenagers who have more wisdom than most adults.

Maturity isn't a number —

it's a mindset.

It's a pattern.

It's a way of approaching life that makes everything clearer, calmer, and cleaner.

Maturity is one of the greatest advantages a person can have, because it removes 80% of preventable problems.

• • • •

Maturity Is Not Seriousness—It's Self-Understanding

MATURITY DOESN'T MEAN being strict, somber, boring, or joyless.

It means you understand:

What triggers you

What drains you

What calms you

What tempts you

What hurts you

What supports you

What sabotages you

What you truly need

Maturity is knowing yourself well enough to choose wisely—not perfectly, just wisely.

It's clarity, not rigidity.

Direction, not intensity.
Awareness, not pressure.

• • • •

Maturity Is Doing What's Best for Your Future, Not What's Easiest for Your Feelings

THIS IS THE SIMPLEST definition you'll ever need:
Maturity=choosing your future over your impulses.
Your feelings might want:
Revenge
Validation
Attention
Escape
Distraction
Comfort
Your maturity wants:
Peace
Dignity
Stability
Self-respect
Long-term happiness
Mature people aren't emotionless—they're **responsible with their emotions.**

• • • •

Maturity Is Pausing Long Enough to Avoid a Lifetime of Regret

IMMATURE PEOPLE ACT fast.
Mature people pause.
Because they know the consequence pipeline:

Impulse→action→outcome
Emotion→reaction→mess
Temptation→yes→regret
The pause is the difference between:
"I can't believe I did that" and "I'm proud I didn't do that."
Maturity is simply the ability to create a moment of awareness before you wreck your own peace.

• • • •

Maturity Is Taking Responsibility, Not Blame

BLAME LOOKS BACKWARDS. Responsibility looks forward.
Immature minds blame:
Other people
Circumstances
Parents
Partners
Society
"Luck"
Timing
Mature minds say: "It's on me to change what comes next."
Not because everything's your fault—but because your future is your responsibility.
That shift is adulthood in motion.

• • • •

Maturity Is Saying No Without Feeling Guilty

IMMATURE PEOPLE SAY yes to avoid discomfort.
Mature people say no to protect their peace.
No to pressure.

No to manipulation.
No to unnecessary commitments.
No to shiny objects.
No to chaotic people.
No to impulse.
No to situations that drain them.

Not because they're selfish — but because they understand the cost of abandoning themselves.

Maturity simplifies everything because it removes the need to explain, justify, or apologize for protecting your sanity.

• • • •

Maturity Is Understanding That Most Things Aren't Personal

IMMATURE MINDS TAKE everything as an attack:
Someone's tone.
Someone's mood.
Someone's silence.
Someone's boundary.
Someone's distance.
Someone's choice.

Mature minds understand:
People are dealing with their own stuff
Not everything is about you
Silence isn't rejection
Boundaries aren't punishment
Someone's issue isn't your responsibility
Other people's behavior reflects them, not you

This understanding saves you from so much unnecessary emotional pain.

• • • •

Maturity Is Consistency, Not Drama

IMMATURE PEOPLE RELY on:
- Intensity
- Big promises
- Emotional swings
- Declarations
- Sudden decisions
- Chaotic cycles

Mature people rely on:
- Follow-through
- Patterns
- Steady habits
- Grounded responses
- Stable routines
- Predictable choices

Maturity isn't loud. It's consistent. And consistency is where **trust lives**.

• • • •

Maturity Is Choosing Relationships That Don't Hurt Your Life

IMMATURE PEOPLE CHOOSE:
- Excitement over character
- Validation over compatibility
- Attention over respect
- Intensity over stability
- Fantasy over reality

Mature people choose:
- Calm
- Clarity
- Consistency

Respect
Communication
Kindness
Alignment

Maturity upgrades your standards, your dating life, your friendships, and your self-worth—**automatically.**

• • • •

Maturity Is Doing the Boring Stuff Before It Becomes the Emergency Stuff

MATURE PEOPLE:
Clean as they go
Show up on time
Pay things early
Plan ahead
Keep their space in order
Handle responsibilities steadily
Think about consequences
Do small tasks before they grow teeth
It's not glamorous —but it creates an easy life.

Immature people avoid the boring stuff until it becomes the stressful stuff.
Then they panic.
Then they repeat.
Maturity breaks that cycle.

• • • •

Maturity Is Emotional Regulation, Not Emotional Suppression

SUPPRESSING EMOTIONS is immaturity.

Regulating emotions is adulthood.
Mature people allow feelings but don't act from them.
They say:
"I'm upset—let me pause."
"I'm stressed—let me breathe."
"I'm hurt—let me think."
"I'm angry—let me step back."
"I'm tempted—let me evaluate."
They don't pretend they're calm.
They **create** calm through regulation.

• • • •

Maturity Makes You Proud of Yourself in a Deep, Quiet Way

WHEN YOU START MAKING decisions that protect your peace instead of destroy it…

When you start choosing clarity instead of chaos…
When you start thinking long-term instead of emotionally…
When you start acting like the future matters…
You build a steady, quiet pride in yourself.
A pride that feels like:
"I handled that well."
"I didn't abandon myself."
"I made the right choice."
"I'm becoming someone I respect."
"I'm not who I used to be."
That is the real **reward** of maturity.

CHAPTER 26—Healing: Rewriting the Effects of Your Old Choices and Building a Clean Slate

Healing is not about becoming perfect.
It's not about forgetting the past.
It's not about pretending things didn't hurt.
It's not about magically erasing consequences.
Healing is about understanding your past well enough that it can't control your future anymore.
Most people think healing is emotional, spiritual, or philosophical.
But healing is also practical.
Healing is cause and effect.
Healing is pattern recognition.
Healing is choosing differently now so your future isn't shaped by your past.

• • • •

Healing Begins With Honest Awareness—Not Self-Blame

HEALING DOESN'T START with:
Guilt
Shame
Beating yourself up
Punishing yourself
Blaming yourself
Healing starts with:
Noticing the pattern
Naming the wound
Acknowledging the consequences

Admitting what happened
Recognizing how you coped
Understanding how it shaped you
Awareness is not judgment—it's clarity.
And clarity is the beginning of freedom.

• • • •

Healing Requires You to Stop Running From What Hurt You

AVOIDANCE IS THE OPPOSITE of healing.
You can't heal from:
What you deny
What you avoid
What you pretend is "fine"
What you numb
What you minimize
What you joke about
What you distract yourself from
What you bury under busy schedules or new people
You don't need to relive the pain—but you do need to acknowledge its impact.
Healing requires honesty, not excavation.

• • • •

Healing Is Not Undoing the Past—It's Understanding It

YOU CAN'T GO BACK BUT you can learn.
Healing means:
"That situation shaped me, and I see how."
"That choice taught me something."
"That pain changed me in ways I can understand now."

"That pattern makes sense based on who I was at the time."
"I don't have to repeat this anymore."
Healing doesn't rewrite history. It rewrites patterns.

• • • •

Healing Is Choosing Present You Over Past You

YOUR OLD SELF MADE choices:
 For survival
 Out of fear
 With limited information
 With low self-worth
 Based on emotional wounds
 From loneliness or pressure
 Without long-term vision
 Your healed self makes choices:
 With clarity
 With self-respect
 With awareness
 With boundaries
 With maturity
 With long-term thinking
 Healing is the shift from surviving to living.

• • • •

Healing Requires Letting Go of the Identity Built from Pain

SOMETIMES THE HARDEST part of healing is giving up the identity you built to cope.
 The identity that says:
 "I'm not worth much."

"I always pick the wrong people."
"I don't deserve good things."
"I'm broken."
"I'm too damaged."
"I can't trust anyone."
"This is just how I am."

Those identities were *protective*—they helped you survive. But healing means outgrowing them. **You're not discarding your past self—you're letting them rest.**

• • • •

Healing Happens When You Stop Repeating What Hurt You

HEALING IS NOT CRYING it out.

Healing is not journaling.

Healing is not reading quotes online.

Those help—but they aren't the transformation.

True healing is when you start making choices that don't recreate old pain.

Healing looks like:

No longer chasing the same kind of person

No longer tolerating disrespect

No longer abandoning yourself to keep someone

No longer numbing instead of dealing

No longer choosing chaos because it feels familiar

No longer reenacting old wounds in new situations

Healing is changing your behavior, not just your feelings.

• • • •

Healing Requires You to Forgive Yourself for What You Didn't Know Then

YOU MADE CHOICES WITH:
The awareness you had
The maturity you had
The guidance you had
The self-worth you had
The coping skills you had
The patterns you had learned
The emotional regulation you hadn't yet developed

Self-forgiveness isn't excusing your past—**it's releasing yourself from dragging it forward**. You can't grow while resenting who you used to be.

Forgive yourself.
Learn the lesson.
Let the past version of you off the hook.

• • • •

Healing Is Slow, Subtle, and Often Unnoticeable in Real Time

HEALING RARELY FEELS dramatic.
It feels like:
Choosing not to respond
Walking away
Staying calm
Saying no
Losing interest in chaos
Desiring peace more than intensity
Respecting yourself
Breaking your own patterns
Noticing red flags earlier

Catching yourself before a bad decision

Healing is a gentle shift in the direction you choose. **You realize you're healing when the same situation doesn't get the same reaction.**

• • • •

Healing Isn't Linear—It's Layered

YOU'LL THINK YOU'RE done healing and then something will trigger an old wound. That doesn't mean you failed. It means you've reached the next layer.

Each layer brings:
More clarity
More awareness
More maturity
More control
More grounding

Healing is not a straight line—it's a staircase. And every step counts.

• • • •

Healing Is a Daily Choice to Protect Your Future From Your Past

HEALING ISN'T A ONE-time transformation.
It's a repeated choice:
"I don't behave like that anymore."
"I don't choose people like that anymore."
"I don't abandon myself anymore."
"I don't repeat that pattern."
"I don't live in survival mode anymore."
"I don't treat myself like I don't matter."

Healing is the commitment to your future self over your old wounds.

• • • •

Healing Builds Self-Respect—And Self-Respect Changes Everything

WHEN YOU HEAL, YOU stop:
- Chasing what hurts
- Tolerating less
- Explaining yourself
- Repeating dysfunction
- Accepting chaos
- Abandoning your needs

And you start:
- Choosing stability
- Protecting your peace
- Walking away faster
- Trusting yourself
- Valuing your time
- Respecting your feelings
- Aligning your actions with your identity

Healing strengthens your standards because you finally understand your worth.

CHAPTER 27—Emotional Independence: How to Stop Giving Other People Control Over Your Life

Most people live emotionally attached to the reactions, moods, opinions, and behaviors of others. Not because they want to—but because they never learned another way.

They learn to feel okay only when:
Someone approves
Someone validates
Someone stays
Someone applauds
Someone agrees
Someone praises
Someone reassures
Someone chooses them
Someone "keeps the peace"

But that makes your emotional life a hostage situation. Emotional independence changes everything. It gives you stability that no one can yank out from under you.

• • • •

Emotional Independence Isn't "Not Caring"—It's Not Being Controlled

PEOPLE MISUNDERSTAND this concept.
Emotional independence is NOT:
Shutting down
Being cold
Avoiding relationships

THE CAUSE AND EFFECT SURVIVAL GUIDE

Being unbothered about everything
Never needing support
Acting like nothing hurts
No.

Emotional independence simply means: **You determine your emotional state—not someone else's behavior.** That's it. It's self-ownership.

• • • •

Dependent Emotions Are Reactive Emotions

WHEN YOU'RE EMOTIONALLY dependent, your emotional state depends on:
    Someone's mood
    Someone's attention
    Someone's approval
    Someone's tone
    Someone's actions
    Someone's inconsistency
    Someone's validation
Your feelings swing with other people's choices.
If they're good to you—you feel good.
If they're distant—you fall apart.
If they approve—you rise.
If they disapprove—you sink.
That is emotional instability disguised as attachment.

• • • •

Emotional Independence Gives You Emotional Stability

WHEN YOU ARE EMOTIONALLY independent:

You stay steady when someone else is moody
You stay calm when someone else is chaotic
You stay grounded when someone pulls away
You stay confident when someone disapproves
You stay respectful even when someone disrespects
You stay aligned when someone pressures
You stay clear when someone manipulates
You stay you — regardless of them

You don't mirror people's behavior. You don't collapse under inconsistency. You don't negotiate your worth with someone else's opinion.

Your emotions belong to YOU.

• • • •

Emotional Independence Comes From Internal Validation

EMOTIONALLY DEPENDENT people need reassurance from the outside. Emotionally **independent** people give reassurance to themselves.

Internal validation sounds like:
"I'm proud of how I handled that."
"I know my intentions."
"I choose what's right for me."
"That opinion doesn't define me."
"I'm allowed to say no."
"I can hold my boundaries."
"I trust my judgment."
"I don't need approval to make good choices."

When you validate yourself, other people lose the power to destabilize you.

• • • •

Emotional Independence Means Not Taking Everything Personally

MOST OF WHAT PEOPLE do has nothing to do with you.
   Their:
   Mood
   Tone
   Distance
   Reaction
   Inconsistency
   Rudeness
   Avoidance
   Silence

...is simply a reflection of **their** insecurities, stress, immaturity, or emotional wounds. Emotional independence recognizes: **"Not everything is about me."** That one sentence saves you from unnecessary suffering.

• • • •

Emotional Independence Requires Boundaries—Real Ones

BOUNDARIES ARE NOT ultimatums.
   They're not punishments.
   They're not manipulation.
   A boundary is simply: **"This is the behavior I accept, and this is the behavior I walk away from."**
   Emotionally dependent people tolerate too much because they fear losing connection. Emotionally independent people protect themselves because they understand the cost of self-abandonment.
   Boundaries aren't walls —they're guardrails.

• • • •

Emotional Independence Isn't Isolation—It Improves Relationships

EMOTIONALLY **dependent** people:
- Cling
- Smother
- Over-give
- Over-share
- Read into everything
- Fear confrontation
- Lose themselves
- Tolerate too much
- Settle
- Break their own boundaries

Emotionally **independent** people:
- Communicate clearly
- Don't play games
- Say what they mean
- Respect other people's autonomy
- Allow space
- Hold their standards
- Stay grounded
- Listen
- Stay honest
- Maintain their identity

Emotional independence makes relationships healthier because you're not using someone as your emotional life raft.

• • • •

Emotional Independence Means You Don't Need People to Choose You to Feel Chosen

THIS IS A BIG ONE.

Most emotional pain comes from wanting someone to:
Pick you
Prioritize you
Pursue you
Validate you
Fix things
Soothe you
Rescue you

But when you're emotionally independent, you understand: "I already choose myself. Anyone else choosing me is a bonus — not the foundation."

That keeps you strong in dating, friendships, family, and even breakups.

• • • •

Emotional Independence Makes You Untouchable to Manipulation

PEOPLE CAN'T EMOTIONALLY control someone who:
Doesn't need external validation
Isn't afraid of being alone
Doesn't crumble under guilt
Doesn't depend on approval
Doesn't react to pressure
Doesn't fear rejection
Emotional independence is the antidote to:
Guilt-tripping
Gaslighting

Love-bombing
Emotional blackmail
Inconsistent affection
Hot/cold behavior

You can't be manipulated when your emotional stability is internally regulated.

• • • •

Emotional Independence Turns Loneliness Into Solitude

WHEN YOU'RE EMOTIONALLY **dependent**, being alone feels like abandonment.

When you're emotionally **independent**, being alone feels like:
Peace
Freedom
Clarity
Space to think
Protection
Calm

Loneliness becomes solitude a solitude becomes strength. **Strong people choose relationships from desire—not desperation.**

• • • •

Emotional Independence Makes You More Attractive

PEOPLE FEEL IT.
They sense:
Your boundaries
Your self-respect
Your calm
Your clarity

Your emotional space
Your stability
Your maturity
Your lack of neediness
You stop chasing—and start choosing.
You stop clinging—and start evaluating.
You stop shrinking—and start standing tall.
It changes everything.

• • • •

Emotional Independence Is the Graduation Level of Emotional Growth

IT COMBINES:
Self-respect
Boundaries
Self-control
Maturity
Healing
Responsibility
Stability
Long-term thinking
Identity

It's the level where you no longer fear losing people because you no longer lose yourself.

CHAPTER 28—Wisdom: Seeing the Long-Term Effects Before You Choose

Wisdom is not age.
Wisdom is not intelligence.
Wisdom is not education.
Wisdom is not being "old enough to know better."
Wisdom is the ability to see the **long-term effect** of a choice before you make it.
People who lack wisdom live in the moment.
People with wisdom live in the moment with the future in mind.
Wisdom is simply consequence-vision.

• • • •

Wisdom Is Foresight—The Skill of Seeing Where a Choice Leads

EVERY CHOICE IS A ROAD. Wisdom lets you see the end of the road instead of staring only at the entrance.
Immaturity only sees:
How something feels now
How exciting it is
How tempting it is
How validating it is
How convenient it is
How fast it feels
Wisdom sees:
The return
The consequence
The pattern
The likely outcome
The emotional cost

The long-term impact
Wisdom lets you see "later" **while** you're still in "now."

• • • •

Wisdom Makes You Slow Down Just Long Enough to Think Clearly

WISE PEOPLE ARE NOT slow —they're strategic.
They pause long enough to ask:
"How does this end?"
"What am I risking?"
"Is this impulse or intention?"
"What is the return on this action?"
"Does this match who I want to become?"
"If I repeat this choice, what life does it build?"
Wisdom is the pause that protects your future.

• • • •

Wisdom Is Pattern Recognition—Not Guessing

YOU DON'T NEED PSYCHIC powers. You need to notice patterns.
People show you:
Who they are
How they behave
How they handle discomfort
How they treat others
How consistent they are
How honest they are
How they act under pressure
What they repeat

And patterns don't lie—even when words do.
Wisdom is trusting the pattern instead of the potential.

• • • •

Wisdom Is Learning From Experience—Yours and Everyone Else's

THE IMMATURE MINDSET says: "I have to do it to learn the hard way."

But wise people pay attention to:
Their own past
Their friends
Their family
People on social media
Stories
Mistakes
Consequences

Wise people don't have to touch a hot stove to know it's hot, they already know it is.

• • • •

Wisdom Is Choosing the Life You Want Later Over What You Feel Now

TEMPTATION SCREAMS. Wisdom whispers.

Temptation pulls you into:
Instant gratification
Emotional decisions
Shiny objects
Impulsive choices
Unsafe people
Shortcuts

Distractions
Wisdom pulls you toward:
Calm days
Clean relationships
Stable routines
Self-respect
Peace
Progress
Emotional safety
Long-term happiness
Wisdom chooses "later" over "right now."
Not to punish yourself—to **protect yourself.**

• • • •

Wisdom Is Understanding That Everything Has a Cost

PEOPLE THINK CHOICES are free until the consequences arrive.
Wisdom sees the cost upfront:
The emotional cost
The mental cost
The time cost
The self-respect cost
The opportunity cost
The peace cost
The consequence cost
Wise people ask: "Is this worth the price?" Most shiny objects aren't.

• • • •

Wisdom Is the End of Excuses

WHEN YOU DEVELOP WISDOM, excuses stop working.
You can't lie to yourself as easily.
You can't pretend you didn't know.
You can't act shocked by the outcome.
You can't keep repeating cycles "accidentally."
Wisdom gives you too much clarity to hide behind excuses. With wisdom, you see yourself honestly—and choose accordingly.

• • • •

Wisdom Makes Your Life Easier Because You Stop Making It Harder

THE WISEST PEOPLE AREN'T perfect—they just avoid unnecessary problems.
They don't:
Get involved with the wrong people
Create emotional drama
Make impulsive choices
Procrastinate until disaster
Ignore red flags
Lie to themselves
Choose chaos
Destroy peace for entertainment
Wisdom makes your life smoother not because life becomes easier—but because **you become wiser.**

• • • •

Wisdom Is Built Through Three Practices: Reflection, Observation, and Correction

1. REFLECTION
   You look back at what happened.
   You connect cause and effect.
   You take responsibility without shame.
   Reflection turns mistakes into lessons.
   2. Observation
   You watch patterns—in yourself and others.
   You pay attention to behavior more than words.
   You notice red flags early.
   Observation turns judgment into clarity.
   3. Correction
   You apply what you've learned.
   You adjust your future choices.
   You stop repeating the same pattern.
   Correction turns knowledge into wisdom.
   Together, these three create **maturity, safety, and self-respect.**

• • • •

Wisdom Makes You the Calm Person in the Room

BECAUSE WISDOM GIVES you:
   Perspective
   Patience
   Emotional control
   Long-term thinking
   Clarity
   Standards
   Stability
   People with wisdom don't need to argue or prove themselves.

They don't react to everything.
They don't take everything personally.
They don't feel threatened by other people's behavior.
Wisdom gives you emotional altitude. You rise above what once dragged you under.

• • • •

Wisdom Makes You Proud of Who You Are Becoming

WHEN YOU MAKE CHOICES from wisdom, you feel:
Grounded
Steady
Confident
Self-respecting
Aligned
Mature
Capable
You become someone you trust.
Someone future-you will thank.
Someone younger-you needed.
Someone others quietly admire.
Wisdom is the soft, steady glow of becoming who you were always meant to be.

CHAPTER 29—Peace: Designing a Life With Minimal Chaos and Maximum Clarity

Peace isn't something you find.
 It isn't something someone gives you.
It isn't something that shows up when life finally becomes perfect.
Peace is something you **build**.
Piece by piece.
Choice by choice.
Boundary by boundary.
Peace isn't luck—it's design.

• • • •

Peace Is Not the Absence of Problems—It's the Absence of Unnecessary Problems

LIFE WILL ALWAYS HAVE:
 Challenges
 Stress
 Loss
 Change
 Responsibility
 Disappointment
 Conflict
 You can't remove those.
 But you can remove:
 The chaos you create
 The drama you choose
 The people you entertain

The patterns you repeat
The impulses you obey
The environments you stay in
The shiny objects you chase
Peace is created by removing the chaos you don't need.

• • • •

PEACE BEGINS WITH CLARITY
Peace comes from knowing:
Who you are
What you value
What you will and won't tolerate
What you want to build
What your standards are
What your priorities are
What your boundaries are
What you've outgrown

Confusion creates chaos. Clarity removes confusion. You cannot build peace while living in emotional fog.

• • • •

Peace Requires Low-Drama Environments

YOUR ENVIRONMENT INFLUENCES your mind more than you realize.

If your space is:
Cluttered
Chaotic
Dirty
Noisy
Disorganized

...your mind will be too.
If your social circle is:
Unstable
Dramatic
Draining
Unpredictable
Disrespectful
...your inner life won't stand a chance.

Peace requires you to curate your environment like your wellbeing depends on it—because it does.

• • • •

Peace Requires You to Walk Away From People Who Don't Want It

YOU CANNOT HAVE PEACE while keeping people who thrive on:
Drama
Chaos
Inconsistency
Manipulation
Irresponsibility
Disrespect
Emotional volatility
Crisis cycles
Mind games

They will drag you back into the life you're trying to evolve out of.

You don't need to hate them.
You don't need revenge.
You don't need a speech.
You just need distance.

• • • •

Peace Requires Predictable Habits

IF EVERYTHING IN YOUR life is unpredictable, your peace will be, too.
> **Peace is created by:**
> Consistent sleep
> Consistent routines
> Consistent cleaning
> Consistent follow-through
> Consistent self-care
> Consistent emotional regulation
> Consistent responsibilities
> **Peace grows where consistency is planted.**

• • • •

Peace Requires Safe Internal Dialogue

YOUR MIND SHOULD NOT be your bully. You cannot experience peace while speaking to yourself like an enemy.
> **Peace requires internal conversations like:**
> "You're doing your best."
> "We can figure this out."
> "One step at a time."
> "Breathe."
> "This feeling will pass."
> "You handled that well."
> "You don't need to rush."
> "You're allowed to rest."
> Self-kindness is not softness—**it's stability.**

• • • •

Peace Requires Boundaries—Not Explanations

BOUNDARIES PROTECT peace better than anything else.
They say:
"This doesn't work for me."
"I need space."
"I won't tolerate that."
"I'm not available for this conversation."
"I don't accept being spoken to like that."
"I will leave if this continues."
"My answer is no."
You don't owe anyone a speech. **Boundaries don't require essays—just consistency.**

• • • •

Peace Requires Emotional Control—Not Emotional Suppression

YOU CAN FEEL EVERYTHING **without** reacting to everything.
Peace means:
You pause
You breathe
You think
You step back
You regulate
You respond intentionally
Not repressing emotions—**containing them long enough to choose wisely.**
When you **stop reacting to every feeling** chaos stops winning.

• • • •

Peace Requires Long-Term Thinking

SHORT-TERM CHOICES create long-term chaos.
Long-term thinking creates long-term peace.
When you think ahead, you stop:
Jumping into drama
Dating red flags
Oversharing
Overspending
Taking impulsive risks
Trusting the wrong people
Abandoning your routines
Living by emotion
Peace comes from seeing the outcome before the action.

• • • •

Peace Requires Letting Go of What Isn't Yours

NOT EVERY BATTLE IS yours.
Not every opinion matters.
Not every misunderstanding needs correcting.
Not every comment deserves a response.
Not every conflict needs engagement.
Not every connection is meant to stay.
Immaturity fights every war. **Wisdom** chooses battles wisely. **Peace** chooses almost none.

• • • •

Peace Feels Like Knowing You Can Handle What Comes

PEACE IS NOT FRAGILE.

Peace is not tiptoeing.
Peace is not pretending everything's fine.
Peace is confidence.
Peace is preparedness.
Peace is resilience.
Peace is emotional steadiness.
Peace is trusting yourself.
Peace is the quiet knowing: **"I'm safe in my own hands."**

. . . .

Peace Is the Natural Byproduct of Living Intentionally
WHEN YOU:
Take responsibility
Choose well
Set boundaries
Think ahead
Stabilize your environment
Avoid shiny objects
Regulate emotion
Protect your identity
Value your future
Act with maturity
...peace becomes your default setting.
Not because life got easier—but because **you got wiser.**

CHAPTER 30—Your New Life: Living Intentionally by Choosing The Life You Want and Walking Forward Without Fear

Every choice you've ever made has led you here—to this moment, reading these words, opening your eyes to the one truth most people never learn:

Your life is shaped by your choices and you have the power to choose well.

Not perfectly.

Not flawlessly.

Not without mistakes.

But **intentionally.**

This book wasn't written to impress you. It was written to equip you—so you can build the life people will think you "got lucky" to have.

But luck has nothing to do with it. This is the result of clarity, awareness, maturity, and courage.

Let's put it all together and bring it home.

• • • •

Your New Life Begins With One Core Skill: Choosing With Awareness

YOU NOW UNDERSTAND the real mechanics of life:

Every action returns something

Consequences are predictable

Shiny objects disguise regret

Emotion tries to trick you

Impulse is loud

Wisdom is quiet
Boundaries protect peace
Stability is built, not found
Consistency compounds
Self-control is a superpower
Maturity shifts everything
Healing rewrites patterns
Responsibility returns power
Peace is designed
Emotional independence frees you
Wisdom safeguards your future
When you combine these skills you stop living reactively and start living intentionally.
You build your life instead of stumbling through it.

. . . .

Your New Life Is Built on Intentional Living—Not Perfect Living

"INTENTIONAL" DOES NOT mean rigid. It means "being aligned" with who you want to be.
Intentional living means:
Intentional choices
Intentional habits
Intentional environments
Intentional conversations
Intentional boundaries
Intentional relationships
Intentional self-respect
Intentional internal dialogue
When you live intentionally, you no longer have to:
Untangle chaos
Fix preventable problems

Repair messes
Repeat old patterns
Apologize for impulsive decisions
Rebuild what you destroyed
Live in a fog of regret
Intentional choices build the life you want to experience.

• • • •

Your New Life Has Higher Standards—Without Apology

YOU NO LONGER:
Settle
Tolerate disrespect
Keep unstable people close
Abandon your needs
Accept chaos
Explain your boundaries
Negotiate your identity
Live for validation
Confuse intensity with connection
Choose short-term relief over long-term peace

You have standards now—not because you're "better" but because you finally **know your worth.**

Standards don't push people away—they filter out those who shouldn't have gotten close in the first place.

• • • •

Your New Life Moves Slower—Because Slow Is Smart

YOU THINK BEFORE CHOOSING.
You pause before reacting.

THE CAUSE AND EFFECT SURVIVAL GUIDE

You evaluate before diving in.
You walk away earlier.
You choose calmer people.
You plan ahead.
You protect your time.
You protect your energy.
You protect your future.
Slowness isn't weakness.
Slowness is wisdom.
Slow is smooth.
Smooth is steady.
Steady is powerful.

• • • •

Your New Life Has Less Fear—Because You Trust Yourself

YOU'VE BECOME SOMEONE you can rely on.
Someone who:
Follows through
Sees consequences coming
Resists shiny objects
Can break their own negative patterns
Stays calm in storms
Sets boundaries
Listens to their intuition/future self
Thinks long-term
Holds responsibility
Chooses peace
Walks away when needed
When you trust yourself fear loses its grip.
Fear can't control someone who knows how to choose well.

• • • •

Your New Life Makes Regret Rare

NOT GONE—RARE.

> **Regret becomes:**
> Small
> Infrequent
> Less dramatic
> Easier to repair
> Less defining
> Less consuming
> **Because you aren't living in reaction mode anymore.**
> You make choices with your eyes open.
> You don't walk into fire thinking it won't burn you.
> You see the cost before paying it.
> You don't confuse temptation with opportunity.
> You don't live blindfolded.
> **Regret fades when awareness rises.**

• • • •

Your New Life Begins When You Choose Yourself—Fully

NOT HALFWAY.
> Not conditionally.
> Not only on good days.
> **You choose yourself:**
> When it's hard
> When it's lonely
> When you're scared
> When you're tempted
> When you're tired

When the world pressures you
When old patterns whisper
When shiny objects sparkle
When your emotions flare
When your past tries to pull you back
Choosing yourself isn't selfish—it's essential.
You're the only person who lives your life.
You're the only one who pays the price for your choices.
You're the only one who experiences the consequences.
So you **MUST** be the one navigating your life **with intent.**

• • • •

Your New Life Is Not Perfect—It's Intentional

THERE WILL STILL BE stress.
   There will still be emotion.
   There will still be challenges.
   There will still be hard days.
   There will still be mistakes.
   But you are no longer lost at sea adrift in the storm. You are now a steady ship no longer fearing the storm because **you know how to navigate through it with grace.**

• • • •

You're Not Ending a Book—You're Beginning a Different Life

THIS ISN'T A GRADUATION. It's a departure.
   You're stepping into the world with:
   Clearer vision
   Stronger identity
   Grounded stability

Higher standards
Mature emotional control
Healthy independence
Long-term thinking
Deep self-respect
Intentional habits
intentional choices

This is the life you were meant to live—a life built on cause and effect, awareness, and responsibility.

A life where you choose deliberately.
A life where you stand confidently.
A life where you protect your peace fiercely.
A life where maturity replaces chaos.
A life where regret rarely touches you.
A life that reflects strength, clarity, and wisdom.

The sails have been raised, the course has been plotted and the waters are calm. All that is needed to get this voyage started is **your desire to live by intent instead of chance.**

See you over the horizon!

Also by Kelly Logan

365 Days of Truth Volume 1
365 Days of Truth Volume 2
365 Days of Truth Volume 3
Sense to Soul How To Have A Personal Relationship With God Through Mystical Interpretation of Scripture
The Cause and Effect Survival Guide
The Cause And Effect Survival Guide
Intuition: The Best Friend You Didn't Know You Had

Watch for more at www.betterbyintent.com.

About the Author

Kelly A. Logan is an author and creator who teaches intentional living through cause and effect, not hype or motivation. Her work focuses on decision-making, intuition as biological awareness, and building stability through practical choices. She is the creator of the *Better by Intent* framework.

Read more at www.betterbyintent.com.

www.ingramcontent.com/pod-product-compliance
Lightning Source LLC
Chambersburg PA
CBHW020838160426
43192CB00007B/708